Fieldwork in Local History

Fieldwork
in Local History

W. G. HOSKINS

*Hatton Professor of English History
in the University of Leicester*

FABER AND FABER LIMITED
24 Russell Square, London

First published in 1967
by Faber and Faber Limited
24 Russell Square London W C 1
First published in this edition 1969
Printed in Great Britain by
Latimer Trend & Co Ltd Whitstable
All rights reserved

© *1967, by W. G. Hoskins*

SBN (paper edition) 571 09225 X

SBN (cloth edition) 571 08552 0

Contents

Preface   *page* 11

1. INTRODUCTION TO FIELDWORK   15
   A backwoods parish   15
   Exploring towns   24
   The country landscape   29
   Additional note on Great Yarmouth   33

2. ANGLO-SAXON LANDSCAPES   34
   Old English estates   34
   Domesday Book and fieldwork   40

3. FIELDWORK IN MEDIEVAL HISTORY   48
   The documentary background   48
   Medieval parks and forests   51
   Moated homesteads   54
   Deserted village sites   55
   Medieval river ports   59

4. TOWNS AND VILLAGES   65
   Towns   65
   Urban housing   67
   Urban street patterns   71
   Villages   73

5

Contents

5. PLACE-NAMES AND TOPOGRAPHY   *page* 77

    Place-names on the Norfolk coast   79

    Place-names and ancient churches   85

    Old and new   89

    Other names   92

6. SMALL HOUSES   94

    Probate and other inventories   95

    Glebe terriers   97

    Houses in towns   104

7. FARMSTEADS   107

    Bartonbury   107

    General sources for farm history   111

8. HEDGES AND WALLS   117

    Mapping hedge-banks   118

    Hedge-banks and their flora   124

    Field walls   130

    Why date walls and hedges?   134

9. ROADS AND LANES   136

    Early trackways   136

    Roman roads   138

    Cattle roads   143

    Other roads and lanes   147

10. TWO TOURS   150

    Some fieldwork in Norfolk   150

    Some fieldwork in Somerset   159

11. FAREWELL TO FIELDWORK   170

Index   185

List of Illustrations

after page 64

Great Yarmouth: one of the Rows

An Old English Boundary (Devon)

An Old English Boundary

Maxey church (Northants)

Thorverton (Devon): the old parsonage

List of Maps

I. Parish of Cadbury (Devon) *page* 20

II. Norfolk Coast from Cromer to Yarmouth 81

III. Buckworth (Hunts.) 120–1
Field boundaries *c.* 1700
c. 1835
1945
1963

IV. Bratton Fleming (Devon): ancient hedgebanks 127

V. Linton (West Yorkshire): ancient fields and walls 131

VI. Holme-next-the-Sea (Norfolk) 141
Road and field pattern in 1609

VII. Langport (Somerset) 162–3

VIII. Maxey (Northants): the island of Maccus 173

Preface

A few years ago I wrote *Local History in England* for the guidance and encouragement of local historians all over the country. In it I included two chapters on fieldwork, which merely gave an outline of a very large subject. The present book deals solely with the various kinds of fieldwork, both in towns and in the countryside. I have tried to think of all the sorts of fieldwork the local historian is likely to engage in and others that may not have occurred to him; but I have no doubt that those who have specialized in some small territory will be able to add something to my account here.

The only major omission from the present book is Industrial Archaeology, which I decided to leave out after much thought and more than one change of mind. Although I have done a little in this field, as for example at the fascinating canal settlement of Shardlow on the Trent and Mersey Canal, I am too conscious of the fact that I have not the technical knowledge to make any respectable contribution in this new field and certainly not enough to offer guidance to others. A number of books have appeared in the last two or three years on this subject, and it now has its own *Journal,* started in 1964. I do not always find the treatment of the subject in books and articles completely satisfactory for it seems to me to contain too much economic and business history and not enough about the visible remains, the pure archaeology, of our industrial and commercial past. Indeed I am coming to the conclusion that the best people to write industrial archaeology are engineers and others with a special technological knowledge, provided they are prepared to acquire an adequate knowledge of economic and business history. It is easier, in my view, for an engineer to pick up his history to a satisfactory level than for an historian to acquire a sound knowledge of technology, and without this he cannot hope to write Industrial Archaeology as it needs to be written. Some of the best 'Industrial Archaeology'—though it was not called that then—has appeared in the *Transactions of the Newcomen Society,* and other technical journals. Nevertheless, there are great advances to be made in this new branch of archaeology. So far I have the impression that we are only feeling our way, in a slightly uncertain fashion; and I do not feel I can usefully contribute to this process. Again, as a further excuse for this omission from my book, I could plead that it requires a book to itself and my own treatment could only be superficial as well as lacking in expertise.[1]

It remains to thank a few friends who have helped me over certain patches of ignorance: Dr. Arthur Raistrick, that great authority on Northern England and on the practical side of local history in general; Dr. Max Hooper, of the Nature Conservancy, whose considerable help is very evident in Chapter 8 on Hedges and Walls; Mr. Charles Green and Miss Barbara Green for much help over Norfolk matters; Dr. Robert Newton, who put me right on the nineteenth-century sources for the study of urban housing and street development; and also those adult education tutors, too numerous to name individually, who have kept me abreast of the excellent work being done in their classes, and who have thereby furnished me with authentic material from various parts of England. It is hardly too much to say that adult education classes are one of the most vigorous growing-points for the serious study of local history in this country.

I also wish to thank the *Listener* for permission to reprint two articles from its pages which form the substance of my first chapter. And finally my grateful thanks to Mrs. Susan Digby

[1] Even since these words were written, Mr. J. P. M. Pannell, a civil engineer by training, has filled this gap with *Techniques of Industrial Archaeology* (David & Charles, 1966).

Firth for typing my manuscript so impeccably. As regards my academic friends named above, it should be said that they are not to be held responsible for any controversial opinions or theories I may have expressed. They are not necessarily in agreement with them.

It is occasionally said that in trying to guide local historians into the paths of righteousness and away from the amateurish imbecilities that often marked much of their work in the past, I am in danger of 'taking all the pleasure out of local history'. This would be sad if it were true, but I doubt whether there is the slightest truth in the charge. As my own experience enlarges of the methods and sources and problems of local history, in whatever part of England I may find myself, I have only noticed an increase of pleasure and I believe the same is true for others who keep an inquiring mind and sharp eyes. No doubt I still miss much in field and street, but I have trained myself to see more and more as the years go by. Time's wingéd chariot hurries near, but the enjoyment I found as a schoolboy is not less than it was: indeed, it is greater for it is better informed. And I believe this is true for every explorer in the endless field of English topography.

Melton Mowbray
9 August 1966   *W. G. Hoskins*

Introduction to Fieldwork

A BACKWOODS PARISH

I had the good fortune to be born in a part of England which
had suffered little change over many generations, or indeed
over many centuries, in a small and ancient city with unravished
country all around it. We could reach the fields within ten
minutes' walk in any direction from the town. Holidays were
spent only ten miles from home, in the deep peace of inland
Devon, reached by a carrier's cart which set out from its
traditional inn—the Bull in Goldsmith Street—every Friday
afternoon. This is not prehistory: it was England just after the
First World War.

There was no village where we stayed: only a small manor-
house where the squire's ancestors had lived, so I was told by
my country cousins, since the time of Alfred the Great. I know
now that the squires, who took their name from their estate,
had actually lived there since the time of Henry the Third,
perhaps a little before that. I also know now as an historian,
many years later, that the estate had indeed belonged to Alfred
the Great, as part of a much larger property which he had left
in his will to his younger son, sometime about the year 880. A
farm near by is still called Chilton, *cild tun,* 'the estate belonging
to a son of a royal or noble family.' I do not know how my
cousins came to possess this esoteric piece of information about
Alfred: whether it was derived from a long, oral tradition
or whether it was merely that Alfred was still a father-figure
in that peaceful backwood of South-Western England.

Less than a mile away was a great earthwork on the top of the highest hill for miles around. Inside this hill-fort, though I did not know it then, lay buried a Romano-British temple; and just below it on the south-western slopes of the hill stood a plain little grey church with a Norman font. This was a mystery I could not fathom at the age of twelve or so. Why a Norman font in a fifteenth-century church?

The church stood almost alone. Near it was the school where my cousins went in the early years of this century, a smithy, and a farm called Church Farm. All the other farms of the parish—some twenty or so—were scattered about the warm combes or on the sheltered hillsides, joined to each other by an intricate pattern of deep and winding lanes, wide enough for one cart and no more (Map I).

I puzzled over the meaning of this landscape, for like most people I regarded villages as the normal kind of settlement in the countryside. Had there ever been a village here and had it disintegrated into scattered farms at an early date? How old were these farms? How had the complicated pattern of lanes and cart-tracks come into existence? What did the entry in Domesday Book mean in terms of the actual landscape as I saw it? And why so often did farmsteads come in pairs, called Higher and Lower—such as Higher and Lower Uppincott, Higher and Lower Endacott, Higher and Lower Chapeltown? Other questions came to me at intervals in later years.

I used to come home from these holidays and get histories of Devon out of the public library, but they never answered my questions or even seemed aware that such questions might be asked. I pored over the one-inch map for hours, trying to read it like a document written in a foreign language, but I got nowhere with it. Yet I remained convinced that it would tell me a great deal if only I could find the key.

Similarly I kept on tackling the translated text of Domesday Book for Devon, hoping that some light would suddenly flash upon that cryptic shorthand text if I went back to it often enough. I felt, as with the ordnance map, that it was in its own mysterious way describing the country landscape I knew and that all the farms I knew on the ground were probably mentioned there in some way. Domesday devoted about a dozen lines to the two manors that lay within that remote parish, but they were all more or less unintelligible to me then.

Books about Domesday did not help. They did not answer the questions I had in mind. Yet I was certain again that Domesday was a kind of guide book to England at the close of the eleventh century; and I know now that it is so. It gives more detail in some parts of the country than others: at times it is virtually useless as a topographical description, at others it is full of information about the country landscape nine centuries ago.

When I was fifteen I found Maitland's *Domesday Book and Beyond* in the public library. I did not get far in my wrestlings with this great work. But Maitland did make a couple of tantalizing remarks early on, and failed to enlarge upon them. At one point he said: 'We are learning from the ordnance map (that marvellous palimpsest which . . . we are beginning to decipher . . .).' And at the foot of the next page he said in another throw-away line or two: 'Much remains to be done before we shall be able to construe the testimony of our fields and walls and hedges . . .'

Maitland's words confirmed what I already thought: that the ordnance map was the most rewarding single document we could have for the study of English topography, and that fields, walls, and hedges were all saying something about the past if only one could decipher the language (see Chapter 8 below). But he gave no further clues to this language of the map and the landscape, and later historians never bothered to follow up these pregnant sentences.

These problems of farmsteads and field-patterns; of hedge-banks, boundaries and lanes; of church and earth-work; of manor-house and woodlands, occupied my mind just about forty years ago, and I began making notes—though not very usefully. They were the first of a long series of questions on English topography that have occupied me from time to time ever since. I answered some of them recently in a book entitled *Provincial England,* more particularly in an essay on 'The Highland Zone in Domesday Book.' Though mostly an interpretation of Domesday as it relates to Devon, some of the conclusions apply equally to other parts of the Highland Zone in England, most of all perhaps to the Welsh border country where the one-inch map of Herefordshire strongly suggests a landscape history similar to that of Devon. So, forty years later, using various kinds of evidence and not least that of my own eyes (and conversations with farmers on the spot), I have answered some of the questions I used to ask in vain of other books.

I was able to show in *Provincial England* that all those scattered farms in Devon had been there just like that as long ago as 1086, when Domesday Book was compiled, and therefore for some time before that—probably back to the middle decades of the seventh century when the Saxons plodded into Devon and took over all the rich lands of the New Red Sandstones.

Church Farm, beside the parish church of Cadbury, had been the lord's demesne farm as long ago as the Norman Conquest, and I was able to define its ancient boundaries with a high degree of precision. In the tithe award of 1842 it contained 95½ acres; but there were three other fields then belonging to another farm, totalling some 12½ acres, which from their location must originally have belonged to Church Farm. This brought the area of the demesne farm to 108 acres, the one virgate of Domesday Book. Its ancient boundaries stood revealed as being lanes on three sides, together with a stream as part of the western boundary; and on the fourth or southern side a straight hedge-bank connected the end of a boundary lane to the stream. So one got back to the proof that these lanes existed when the demesne farm was first created, and to the approximate date of the southern boundary hedge-bank.[1]

The other farms in the parish could be identified as those of the villeins who are enumerated in Domesday. There had never been a village here. The isolated farm is the aboriginal mode of human settlement over most of Devon; and the lanes are very often the boundaries of these ancient farms. Either they had existed when these farms were first colonized from the natural landscape, or, more probably, they were dug out as

[1] For the identification of demesne farms in South-West England in 1086 see *Provincial England* pp. 23-4, 25-6, 31-3, and 46-7.

double-ditches in order to produce artificial boundaries between one farm and another where there were no natural features to help in fixing bounds. Not all lanes and tracks originated in this way, but a considerable proportion did so. Since they were hand-made by peasants, or even by slave-labour, hacked and dug out by axe, mattock, and spade, they avoided natural obstacles on the ground (large trees, boulders, marshy ground), and thus, with steep slopes as well to contend with, produced the narrow winding deep-set pattern of lanes so striking upon the map and upon the ground itself.

As for the earthwork in this parish of my early explorations, it turned out to have had a Romano-British temple in the centre of the oval fortress, and third-century coins have been found in the track leading up to it. Later, a Christian church, dedicated to St. Michael, was built on the south-western slopes of the hill, about 350 yards below the earthwork. Michael is a favourite dedication for a hill-top church. It is likely that this church, though not planted exactly on the pagan site as in some places, was a deliberate successor to the older sacred site. Such a superimposition was not uncommon in the missionary days of Christianity in a hostile countryside.

Whether there was a gap between the use of the heathen temple at Cadbury and the first Christian worship we shall never know, but Christianity had certainly reached Exeter, only ten miles away, by the fourth century. The tradition of pagan worship on this site may well have lingered on long enough for a later religion to take it over. Perhaps this is why, too, the rural deanery—an ancient institution in itself— is named after this small and undistinguished church and not after one larger and more obviously important. All these bits of evidence, not conclusive in themselves, fit together to form a pattern of human continuity in this small piece of landscape.

Now we move back into uncharted territory. Third-century coins and a late Roman temple or shrine imply habitations not far away, and habitations imply farming. So the farms which I showed to have existed well back in Saxon times may themselves have taken over from farmsteads going back to Iron

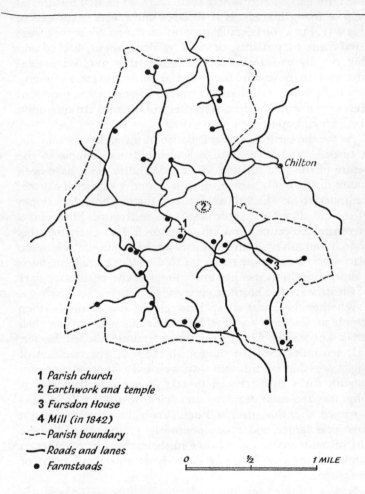

1 *Parish church*
2 *Earthwork and temple*
3 *Fursdon House*
4 *Mill (in 1842)*
-·-- *Parish boundary*
── *Roads and lanes*
● *Farmsteads*

0   ½   1 MILE

MAP I **Parish of Cadbury** (Devon) Showing farmsteads and lane pattern, nearly all established by the eleventh century and much
of it earlier.

Age times, when the earthwork was first constructed (*c.* 100 B.C.) as a measure of protection. The relationship between the modern farms and those of Saxon times has been established; but I have yet to work out—if it is ever going to be possible— the relationship between the Saxon farms and those of Romano-British and earlier times. I think the necessary evidence may be forthcoming one day through archaeologists and air-photographs. In the meantime, I am convinced that in some of the fertile parts of Devon, and in many fertile parts of England such as the Vale of Evesham, the evidence is mounting for an unbroken continuity of farming from prehistoric times to the present day.

In walking round the countryside, looking at individual farms with Domesday in mind, I became interested also in the structure of the existing farm-houses and the lay-out of the whole farmstead as a complex of buildings. These are two distinct, though possibly related, fields of inquiry.

Even when a particular farm is known to have existed for over a thousand years, as one can sometimes say from the evidence of a Saxon land-charter, no structure remains standing above ground which is anything like as old as this. There are primitive and abandoned dwelling-houses on Dartmoor, built of imperishable granite, which may well date from the thirteenth century, and some certainly from the fourteenth; but in the lowlands, where houses were built of less durable materials, it is rare to find much secular building that is older than about 1400.

What I did find, exploring old farmhouses all over England, was that an extraordinary number of them—in all counties except the extreme north—had been rebuilt or extensively modernized in the late sixteenth century or the early seventeenth. There were again no books to tell me how to date these structures. Though there were, and are, plenty of books instructing one in the dating of churches and their individual features, no one had made an intensive study of what one might call 'ordinary buildings' in the towns and in the countryside and how to date them. I had to teach myself by observing dated buildings, taking care that the date related to the main

21

structure and not to some minor repair or to some domestic event (such as the marriage of a young couple who then took over a family house and put their own happy date above the door). One learnt to date houses from mouldings in ceiling-beams, or over doorways and windows, or most of all by types of roof structure. Sometimes a house contained more than one period of building: perhaps two or three: and its structural history could be as complicated as that of a parish church.[1]

The Great Rebuilding, as I termed it, that occurred in England between about 1570 and 1640, both in towns and in the countryside, was nowhere documented. The evidence was almost entirely in the field. It is a good example of purely visual evidence, telling us about important social changes—the modernizing and enlargement of houses at nearly every social level—that was so commonplace while it was happening that no one bothered to record it on paper.

Once the phenomenon was recognized, it was then possible to turn back to certain documents—made for quite another purpose—to trace the growth in the size and complexity of ordinary houses during the sixteenth century and the early seventeenth. These documents are probate inventories, which list more or less carefully the entire personal estate of a dead person for the purpose of proving and administering his or her last will and testament. At their best these records list every room in the dead man's house, with all their contents, and so enable us to see houses growing from simple medieval dwellings of two or three rooms at most to more elaborate structures of six to eight, or even ten rooms occasionally. The documents often give a name to every room, and so amplify and explain what the structures alone do not tell us. Moreover, they enable us to place houses in their social class, so to speak. We can distinguish in the countryside the houses of labourers, of husbandmen and craftsmen, of parsons (both rich rectors and struggling vicars) and of top yeomen. In the towns we can distinguish the houses of labourers (not many), of artisans and shop-keepers, of merchants great and small. And we can, of

---

[1] The publication of Maurice Barley's book on *The English Farmhouse and Cottage* (1961) has made the study of vernacular building much easier since then.

course, distinguish all these houses at different periods of time as well as by social class.[1]

One thing even these documents do not tell us about, and that is the overall plan of a complex unit such as a farmstead, or a big merchant's house and its ancillary buildings. Here we have to go back to the ground itself and study the surviving structures, and observe the relationship of the different buildings within the complex to each other. For farmsteads this is particularly revealing and important. We need plans of the whole site and not merely of the dwelling-house, for there are numerous varieties of plan and they all tell us something for which we have no written record. Similarly with the complex sites of former merchant-businesses in some of our old towns like King's Lynn and Ipswich. These sites are particularly vulnerable to modern methods of destruction since they usually stand in old, crowded and narrow streets.

What started for me, as a schoolboy then, simply as a vague, unformed interest in 'old buildings' has turned out to be an invaluable mass of historical evidence—evidence for important social and economic changes which are otherwise unrecorded or recorded only so indirectly as to escape notice altogether. Like the ordnance map, houses at all social levels and in all periods speak their own testimony of the past if only we can construe it. And this, of course, is equally true of houses being built now. As a social historian I observe their plan, their disposition of rooms and the relative importance of the rooms, with an acute interest. The decline of the dining-room into a miserable annex known (horribly enough) as a 'dinette', and the corresponding rise in importance of the garage or the 'carport', reflect the fact that to a great number of people today the car is vastly more important than good food. The car is run on the housekeeping money, and the plan of the modern house reveals it. In the same way one can trace the social habits of ordinary people from the ruins of thirteenth-century farmhouses on Dartmoor, or from Elizabethan farmhouses in Suffolk, and at every period of time since.

[1] For the Great Rebuilding and the evidence behind it, structural and documentary, see my *Provincial England*, pp. 131–48.

Vernacular Building—as it is now called—presents us with a tremendous body of material evidence for the economic and social history of this country, and for the local history of every parish and town. In 'vernacular building' I include the parish church, which has a great deal to tell us that has yet to be deciphered. There are shelves of books on the English Parish Church, but there is still much to be discovered and put down in print about it, for it is as vernacular, speaking its own language peculiar to the district, as the neighbouring farmhouse or barn or mill.

EXPLORING TOWNS

Most of my exploring has been done in the country, rather than in towns, but not entirely. I have lived in three ancient towns—Exeter, Leicester, and Stamford—and would have been blind if I had not explored them all minutely. And I have explored other special towns, seeing evidence in their lay-out and their buildings that is nowhere recorded in books or documents. Probably every town is a special case. But it must be explored on foot. The car is useless in this kind of inquiry; and so too are air photographs. They tell less than can be got from a good nineteenth-century town map. By unravelling the town plan—the way the streets run in relation to each other or to some central feature like a river, a market-place, or a mother-church—one learns a kind of history that is not otherwise recorded, the way in which the town developed as a physical organism.

I remember being puzzled for years when I lived in Stamford about why the Great North Road, one of the main arteries of England before the railways, should make a number of abrupt bends—two of them right-angled bends—as it went through the old centre of the town. Nothing could have been more illogical for such an ancient road. Eventually I spotted the clue when walking in the town one morning along the street called Scotgate, the street by which the road leaves Stamford for the north. Coming towards the town I noticed that the beautiful spire of St. Mary's—the mother-church of the town since the middle of the seventh century—lay straight ahead of me some distance away, though to get to it I had to make all these bends in the main road. It then came to me that the Great North Road must once have run on a straight course past St. Mary's and then straight down to the old ford—the 'stone ford'—that gave the town its name. What had caused it to deviate in such a fashion from its original logical course?

Domesday Book supplied the answer, though not in an immediately intelligible form. It described a place called Portland, not easily identifiable. The name meant simply *portland,* the land belonging to a *port* or market. It mentioned two churches—St. Peter's and All Saints—and a meadow. These clues could have fitted Northampton, as well as Stamford, but the Domesday entry came immediately after that of Great Casterton, the next village to Stamford along the Great North Road. So Portland was in fact the new market-place set up just outside the Saxon town of Stamford, perhaps just after the Norman Conquest when several towns were enlarged into two boroughs known as the French borough and the English borough as at Nottingham, or the old town and the new town, as at Northampton.

All the clues on the ground and in the documents fitted my theory about Stamford perfectly. A large new market place had been set up immediately to the west of the Saxon town, and two new churches built, one at each end; All Saints still stands in the market-place, but St. Peter's is now marked only by a grassy space. This big new development altered the street-plan of the old town, since it attracted people and traffic towards it. The old North Road, instead of pursuing a straight course over Stamford bridge, past St. Mary's church, and so towards Scotland, now made an abrupt turn westwards towards the busy new market-place, thus creating the first of the right-angled bends which survives to this day. Other old streets, such as the High Street, were also aligned on the new market-place. In fact the topography of the old town was radically altered. New streets came into existence near the market on what was formerly open land, so creating yet other sharp bends in the road. Bit by bit the topographical changes made in the eleventh

and twelfth centuries could be pieced together, all from noticing in the first place a particular alignment of an old church on
the ground.

Take another special town: Great Yarmouth has—or had
before the war—a unique town plan. There were three main
streets running roughly north and south along the old sandbank on which the original town grew up in the Anglo-Saxon
period. Crossing these main streets and joining them together
were no fewer than 156 narrow lanes. These were known as
'the Rows' (frontispiece). Though heavily bombed during the
last war, enough of this remarkable plan survives to make it
worth exploring. But what is the meaning of it, for no other
town in England adopted this plan? There are two tenable
theories. Yarmouth was in medieval times one of the biggest
towns in England, and the point of entry into the richest
region in the country. It was also a frontier town, for many
invaders have made their initial attack on the East Anglian
coast. Indeed, even in 1940 the Germans were thought by
us to be planning their invasion for the East Anglian coast
rather than by the shortest crossing over the straits of Dover.
Anyone who captured medieval Yarmouth would have possessed one of the keys of England.

The town was walled around in the latter half of the thirteenth
century. I noticed that the Rows all stop short of the walls, for
obvious military reasons, and I was inclined to connect the
building of this close pattern of narrow lanes with the building
of the walls, which could be dated. It would have been almost
impossible to capture a town with so much street-fighting
involved in the days before aerial obliteration. So much for the
military theory.

The other theory is perhaps a better one. We know that the
town started life on a sandbank and was colonized by fishermen. The basic land requirements of such an economy were a
strip of foreshore on which boats could be drawn up, together
with an area of higher ground behind it for a hut and perhaps
a garden. At Yarmouth this produced a pattern of parallel land
holdings on the lee or western side of the sandbank. But the
River Yare was not stable in its course and eventually built up

another beach-line farther to the west, and then—later still—
yet another beach-line beyond that. Each of these old beach-
lines is marked by what is now a significantly curving main
street. As the foreshore moved westward in this fashion the
fishing colony moved to the new beach-line, so extending the
original pattern of strips divided by narrow lanes and eventually
producing the three main streets and the whole astonishing pattern that survived until the nineteen-forties.

There is some supporting evidence for this theory of the
lay-out of Yarmouth. The first is documentary: records of the
twelfth century seem to suggest that the Rows, or some of
them, existed even then, before the walls were built. If this
evidence is sound, it would seriously weaken the military
theory. Secondly, I am told one can see this basic pattern
repeated in Malayan fishing villages to this day, though one
would like a few more ethnographic parallels. And, thirdly,
a close watch of deep trenching in Great Yarmouth, in this
older part of the town, suggests that the archaeological and
stratigraphical evidence fits this theory that the river has
created successive beach-lines since the first fishing-settlement
perhaps 1,300 years ago, and that these three successive beach-
lines have directly and indirectly produced the street-pattern of
Great Yarmouth.[1]

There is a whole book—several books—to be written about
the physical growth of towns. In my explorations I have always
remembered a good aphorism: 'Cities do not grow: they are
built'. This statement keeps one's feet firmly on the ground in
working out the evolution of a particular town-shape and
street-plan. Indeed, in walking about old towns, one develops
a peculiar sensitivity in the soles of one's feet. At Great Yarmouth one can feel underfoot the shape of the sandbank cast
up by the sea in post-Roman times on which the first fishermen
put up their huts and on which they dried their herring nets. In
other places I can feel the shape of the open heathland on which
the town first began, as at Hedon in east Yorkshire or Wymondham in Norfolk. I see nothing odd or unexpected in this,
though one can sometimes be misled. It is only the parallel to

See the additional note at the end of this chapter.

the surgeon's sensitive fingers as he probes gently, feeling hidden evidence that is beyond the knowledge of one without his experience.

The plan of Great Yarmouth was unique and has now been largely destroyed: though what is left is worth seeing. Totnes in South Devon keeps its untouched plan: not a street has been destroyed. What makes it particularly rewarding to the explorer and the topographer is that it retains also dozens of narrow sidepassages, each one different in character, joining one street to another, running alongside the elongated medieval and Elizabethan houses and their gardens to a great depth. Totnes is so good that it would repay a house-by-house study while there is yet time. Now that the Ministry of Housing and Local Government is waking up to the fact that our historic towns are being obliterated—not just a good house here and a good house there, but whole streets at a time—and talks about preserving some of these historic centres as a whole and as intact as possible, Totnes should be at the top of any list. Here is a town of Anglo-Saxon foundation, whose basic shape has been determined by the earthen ramparts of the tenth century, whose pattern of streets and lanes is partly Saxon and partly medieval and little else: it would be easy to save it as it is. This is the way to teach children history, not just from books.

The urban pattern made by Ware in Hertfordshire is another very striking one. Visually, there is the beautiful stretch of malthouses, gardens, and tree-shaded summerhouses backing on to the river Lea—one of the most appealing river-scenes in any English town. And topographically, looking at the first (coloured) edition of the 25-inch ordnance map, one sees a very distinctive lay-out altogether: a complete early medieval set-up with the ancient parish church at one end; the High Street curving and varying in width, leading away from it, roughly parallel with the river; and what is so special is that between the High Street and the river there is a series of abnormally long, narrow strips, nearly all occupied by malthouses. It must be the biggest concentration of malthouses anywhere in England. The map, published in 1880—over eighty years old already—is a historical record in itself; and, coloured as it is, it speaks to me like one of those problem or narrative pictures beloved of Victorian painters. Why this remarkable pattern?

Ware is basically a town that established its pattern in the closing years of the twelfth century, crippling the much older town of Hertford just up the river. The bridge indeed first came into the records in 1191, when it was broken by the men of Hertford in an attempt to prevent traffic going that way to the detriment of Hertford. But Ware belonged to the powerful earls of Leicester against whom no parochial squabbling could prevail. The men of Hertford were promptly and heavily fined, and the earl obtained a market for his town of Ware a few years later. At the same time—in 1199 or 1200—he granted it a charter, so creating a borough. Visually, these legal events produced the main elements in the pattern we see today: the huge V-shaped market-place running up to the church, and the long, narrow burgage tenements running southward from the market-place to the riverbank.

The market-place was later encroached upon with buildings, so producing the irregular High Street and the lesser streets behind the encroachments to the north: one can trace all this happening in succeeding centuries. And the vast corn and malt trade, dating from the earliest days of the new borough, gave the town its distinctive architecture. The serried malthouses constituted some of our finest industrial archaeology.[1] Indeed, the whole area between the High Street on the north and the river on the south, westwards to the priory and east to the bridge, should be preserved as one of the historic town centres of England, and protected from the acids of modern development. But, alas, the developer moves faster than any Ministry or any law; and I have no doubt that the ancient pattern of Ware, in all its colour and unique beauty, will become a sacrifice to the great god Mammon.

THE COUNTRY LANDSCAPE

Coming back to the countryside, it was in the 1930s that I found my first deserted medieval village, in the upland pastures

[1] Now (1966) almost entirely destroyed in the interests of 'development'.

of south Leicestershire. I had been attracted to the place by the ruined church and the dried-up moated site not far away; but I had no idea at first that a large village had completely disappeared from the landscape some centuries earlier. In a large grass field near the church I saw extensive markings—humps, ditches, and hollow-ways—which seemed to make a regular pattern, mostly of rectangles separated by narrow lane-like depressions. The 'museum man' who accompanied me on some of my explorations agreed that the whole field seemed to be marked with some man-made earthworks but could not identify them as being like anything he had seen in other periods and places. The meaning of the site remained a mystery until in browsing through Hadrian Allcroft's *Earthwork of England* I noticed a plan of a similar site in Nottinghamshire which was thought to be that of an old village destroyed in a hurricane. Allcroft indeed had a few pages about deserted villages, but economic historians had not read his pages, and though they knew there were thousands of such sites on the Continent they had never thought of looking for them in this country. I have the feeling that *Earthwork of England* is a generally neglected book, and that fieldworkers in local history ought to use it more, even to buy and possess it.

The deserted village I had found by accident was Knaptoft. Once I had identified it by name, I could begin to look for documents. A few medieval records threw light on how large it had once been: an extent of 1268 in the Public Record Office listed a resident lord of the manor, two or three free tenants, 24 villein farmers, and 8 cottagers. The site of the manor house was inside the dried-up moat, but the houses of the freeholders, the villeins, and the cottages all lay beneath the hummocks in that pasture-field, awaiting recognition. Other records (extents, tax assessments, rentals, and so forth) showed the village slowly decaying until it was finally wiped out by large-scale enclosures for sheep and cattle pastures in the early sixteenth century. I began to identify similar sites in empty fields all over Leicestershire. I discovered in all about sixty such sites of deserted villages in exploring the backwoods of Leicestershire, and eventually wrote the first essay on the subject in 1944—'The Deserted Villages of Leicestershire'. I remember writing this during long, boring fire-watching nights in a dreary London office. Though a few local archaeologists had known of some 'lost villages' decades before I re-discovered them, they had paid little or no attention to them, and had usually attributed their disappearance to every reason except the right one. Moreover, they had little idea of the chronology of desertion. When one such site was excavated by amateurs on a Cornish moor in the 1890s they identified the pottery as 'rude British ware' and put the village down as prehistoric. Fortunately the pottery was preserved in a local museum and was re-examined in recent years and found to be mainly of twelfth and thirteenth century date.

When I wrote about the Leicestershire sites, I hazarded the guess that a very great number of deserted villages remained to be identified all over England. I knew of only three or four such sites in Rutland and estimated that there ought to be ten or twelve. We now know of thirteen sites in Rutland. I also thought that a hundred or more sites awaited identification in Northamptonshire and a systematic search in recent years has produced a list so far of eighty-two names. Altogether, just under 2,000 sites of deserted villages are now known from one end of England to the other. A good deal is known also about the causes and chronology of their disappearance. A whole new field of Medieval Archaeology has been opened up. A few excavations are being carried on—notably at Hound Tor in the middle of Dartmoor, a spectacular collection of ruined granite farmhouses and buildings, and at Wharram Percy on the chalk of the Yorkshire Wolds. The first substantial monographs on the lost villages of Oxfordshire and Northamptonshire have now appeared[1], and my essay of twenty years ago on the lost villages of Leicestershire will eventually be superseded, having served its purpose.

Though I find old towns absorbing to work out on the ground, and there is still so much to do and so little done, I

[1] University of Leicester. Department of English Local History: Occasional Papers, no. 17, The Deserted Villages of Oxfordshire (Leicester University Press, 1965) and no. 18, The Deserted Villages of Northamptonshire (1966).

also find myself turning back more and more to the country-side. Ten years ago I summed up most of what I knew then about the history of the English landscape, both country and town, in a book called *The Making of the English Landscape*. Already I could write that book again, doubling its length and correcting a few points; but I prefer for the time being to concentrate upon a small piece of East Anglia, a stretch of the north Norfolk coast between Morston and Sheringham and going back inland for three or four miles—a piece of country that has come to interest me enormously. Every time I go to look at it I see things in it that are significant, or so I believe. I do not always know 'significant of what', but it offers problems to be solved. Here is a landscape of salt marsh, of arable, of heathland and old woods, of market-town and coastal villages, which has been inhabited since mesolithic times. What interests me is the uses to which it has been put at different times, and the interaction between the landscape and the men who have lived in it. I should like to write eventually a human ecology of the north Norfolk coast, helped by an archaeologist and a physical geographer. We roam around it together, asking questions of each other and occasionally finding the answers. Every object in the landscape tells us something, though we are not always sure what it is really saying. I have worked long in the south-west of England, a long time in the east Midlands, and a little in the north; but Norfolk is new country to me, and I see it with fresh eyes and a mind accustomed to a different topography.

We live in a country that is richer than any other in the visible remains of the past. The evidence is so abundant that the major problem is how to organize it into a coherent pattern, and one can only do this by learning to ask the right questions. This evidence has been almost completely ignored by historians, including even the most devoted local historians. Most of us are visually illiterate, and historians as a class are additionally blinded by the belief that only documents are evidence. The material evidence of the past lies all around us, if only we can construe the language it is speaking. In the book that follows I have tried to construe this language; and even if I do not know all the answers (and I do not) I have at least tried to offer clues to the alphabet.

ADDITIONAL NOTE ON GREAT YARMOUTH

Since the pages on Great Yarmouth were written, two further points have emerged in correspondence. Col. C. P. H. Wilson of East Wretham, Thetford, Norfolk, writes: 'You can see the fisherman/sandbank pattern happening every year in Burma on the Irrawady and Chindwin. The banks are covered during the monsoon rains, but when they emerge they are settled by fishermen building their temporary bamboo huts with compounds round them for gardens and storage, and with narrow paths between them for passage. This is the Yarmouth pattern—repeated every year.' Such patterns may well appear in other parts of the world.

The other point was raised by Dr. Adrian Robinson of the University of Leicester. Speaking as a physical geographer, he thought that the successive beach-lines which created the basic street-pattern at Yarmouth were less the result of the instability of the river Yare than of changes in the relative land and sea-levels within historic times. Such a change is well evidenced; for example, all round the shores of the North Sea in the thirteenth century. The Yarmouth sandbank probably emerged permanently from the sea and dried out as a consequence of a recession of the sea, i.e. a relative rise in the land-level, in Middle or Late Saxon times.

Clearly these are complex problems of physical geography which need to be studied closely on the ground. For certain coastal and near-coastal sites the local historian-fieldworker needs the expert assistance of the physical geographer, just as in determining the age of hedgebanks for his local agrarian history he needs the help of the trained botanist.

2

Anglo-Saxon Landscapes

OLD ENGLISH ESTATES

The materials for fieldwork in the distant and obscure Anglo-Saxon period are primarily the great number of land charters referring to grants of estates to various men or monastic institutions, or confirmations of earlier grants; and at the very end of the period the pages of Domesday Book, which give us a more or less detailed picture of most of England towards the end of the eleventh century.

There are many hundreds of surviving land charters from the late seventh century onwards. At their best they set out the boundaries of the estate that is being conveyed, even down to single trees or stones if they happen to form a suitable landmark. The earliest charters do not give boundaries, and those that follow are usually content to specify boundaries in the broadest possible manner. This was sufficient at a time when so little of the countryside had been settled closely. Thus a grant by Aethelbald, king of Mercia, in the year 736, to Ealdorman Cyneberht of land at Stour in Ismere (Worcestershire) describes the estate as 'in the province to which was applied by the men of old the name Ismere, by the river called Stour, with all necessities belonging to it, with fields and woods, with fisheries and meadows. . . . And the aforesaid estate is bounded on two sides by the above-named river, and has on its northern side the wood which they call Kinver, but on the west another of which the name is Morfe, the greater part of which woods belongs to the aforesaid estate.' These boundaries are of the

broadest description. The grant also serves to indicate something of the nature of the country in the first half of the eighth
century, with its suggestion of scarcely touched forests on two
sides of the settled land.

More detailed boundaries are given in a grant made in 958
by King Edgar to his thane Ealhstan of land at Staunton in
Herefordshire: 'And this land is surrounded by these boundaries: First from the mill ford along the Arrow, then to *Washford*;
from *Washford* along the Arrow round the top of *Holneig*; from
the top of *Holneig* to the top of the oak edge, then along the top
of the oak edge, then to the front of the *snaed* way, from the
snaed way round *Hanley* to *aecna*-bridge, up along the brook,
then to the dyke, along the dyke to *Tanesbaec*, from *Tanesbaec*
along the boundary-fence, then to the boundary of the community of *Lene*, along the boundary of the community of *Lene*,
then to AEthelwold's hedge, from AEthelwold's hedge to
Heanoldan, from *Heanoldan* to the boundary thorn, from the
boundary thorn along the fence to the swing-gate, from the
swing-gate along the paved road to the dyke-gate, from the
dyke-gate to the third gate, then along the paved road back to
Milford.'

Even more detailed boundaries are given in a grant in 846
of twenty hides of land in the South Hams of Devon by one
of the kings of Wessex. These are set out as follows:[1] 'These
indeed are the boundaries of these twenty hides in Ham which
his councillors conceded to King AEthelwulf, in the place
which is called Dorchester on the second day of Christmas,
in the presence of suitable witnesses whose names in-
scribed below are made clear to the eyes of beholders: First
into *Mercecumb*, then into the green pit, then on to the tor at
Mercecumbes spring, then to Denewald's stone, then to the ditch
where Esne dug across the road, thence down to the source
of the spring, then down from there by the brook, as far as
Tiddesford, then up the brook as far as Heott's ditch to the
stream, from the stream down where the vixen's ditch meets

---

[1] As given in *English Historical Documents,* vol. I, pp. 482–3. Like most of such
boundaries these are difficult to work out, and all attempts so far have been
unsatisfactory. Yet it could probably be done with sufficient patience and acumen.

the brook, and then down the brook to the sea. Then from Thurlestone up the brook as far as *Mollycombe,* from the head of *Mollycombe* to the grey stone, then up above the source of the spring into *Odencolc,* thence on the old way towards the white stone, thence to the hill which is called "at the holly," thence to the hoary stone, thence to the source of *Secgwell,* thence eastward into the fort, thence westward to the little fort, thence to the paved road, thence below the wood straight out to the reed pool, then up the Avon until the old swine-enclosure runs out to the Avon, then by that enclosure on to a hill, then on to Sorley, thence to the source of "Wolf-well," thence along the "wall-way" to the stone at the stream, from the stone on along the highway to the ditch, thence down to *Wealdenesford,* thence on to the hollow way, thence down the brook to *Hunburgefleot,* and there to the sea.'

Not all the later charters give boundaries. Thus of the eight known land-charters relating to Shropshire between 664 and 975, only two—in 963 and 975—give boundaries. These have been worked out by H. P. R. Finberg in the *Transactions of the Shropshire Archaeological Society,* vol. LVI (1957–8), pp. 28–33. Leicestershire has not a single land-charter which gives boundaries. Of six Rutland charters, only one (for Ayston in 1046) gives boundaries. These are worked out in C. R. Hart, *Early Charters of Eastern England* (1966), pp. 108–9. Thus some parts of England are singularly deficient in materials for this kind of fieldwork; others are rich and offer enough fieldwork for years. According to Dr. T. R. Thomson, in his paper on 'The Saxon Land Charters of Wiltshire' (*Wilts. Archaeological and Natural History Magazine,* vol. LVIII, pp. 442–6) the average time taken to 'solve' a charter is about two years. One of his larger charters (Brokenborough) took four years. The late O. G. S. Crawford took six months over Bedwyn and Burbage in Wiltshire (see *Wilts. A. & N. H. Magazine,* vol. XLI). 'Generally speaking,' continues the same authority, 'the topographer knows at once when he has closed up the bounds satisfactorily. . . . It all "fits" and no doubts remain. Of course, many charters will, for various reasons, never be solved.'

It should be observed, as regards the length of time these

charters take to work out, that in all cases we are referring to the spare-time activities of busy professional men (or busy housewives). Yet even so one can rarely elucidate the boundaries of a sizeable charter in less than many expeditions in the field, a great deal of cogitation over the large-scale maps, and frequent changes of mind.

The present whereabouts of Anglo-Saxon land charters is itself a matter of some difficulty. The standard works by Birch and Kemble are not complete in this respect. Many charters have been discovered since they compiled their great collections. But no modern scholar has attempted to produce an up-to-date collection for the country as a whole. Nevertheless, many counties have been covered in three volumes of *Studies in Early English History* published by the Leicester University Press. Finberg's *Early Charters of the West Midlands* (1961) lists the charters for Gloucestershire, Worcestershire, Herefordshire, and Shropshire, with valuable critical notes and discussions of some charters; and the same scholar's *Early Charters of Wessex* (1964) covers Hampshire, Wiltshire, Somerset, and Dorset. The counties of Devon and Cornwall were covered by Finberg in *Early Charters of Devon and Cornwall* (Occasional Paper, no. 2, Leicester University Press, 1953, revised edition 1963). Thus ten counties on the western side of England have been systematically covered. C. R. Hart's *Early Charters of Eastern England* (Leicester University Press, 1966) deals with Huntingdonshire, Cambridgeshire, Norfolk, Suffolk, Lincolnshire, Rutland, and the Soke of Peterborough. Dr. Hart also covered the county of Essex in two Occasional Papers (Leicester, nos. 10 and 11, 1957) entitled *Early Charters of Essex*. The late Dr. G. B. Grundy dealt with a number of counties in his time, and his papers will usually be found in the historical and antiquarian journals of the county concerned, for example 'The Saxon Charters and Field Names of Somerset' in the *Proceedings of the Somerset Archaeological and Natural History Society* (1927–34).

Dr. Grundy not only listed the charters for various counties but also worked out their boundaries. His work has been much criticised on the ground that he worked mainly from Ordnance maps in his study and many of his 'solutions' to charters are therefore suspect. Though the majority of his solutions are as accurate as anyone could make them, a considerable number need working over again and it would be safer for the local fieldworker to look closely at all Grundy's solutions even though most of them will turn out to be accurate. Grundy was a pioneer in the study of Anglo-Saxon topography, and like all pioneers can be subjected to later criticism by those who have not suffered the pangs of clearing the first path.

Having located a charter containing boundaries, and succeeded in getting it translated into modern English, how does the fieldworker proceed?

Vital though fieldwork is, it is useless to plunge into the depths of the countryside without considerable preparatory work on the map. The best scale for this purpose is the 2½-inch map, which should be sufficient for the first working-out of the boundaries. At a later stage, the 6-inch map may well be called in for greater detail. The one-inch map is quite inadequate for this kind of work.

Since all the boundary points follow in logical order, each being related to the one before it and the one coming after, it is only necessary to identify one certain point—not necessarily the starting-point of the charter—in order to begin work on the map.

The boundary points are generally set out in a clockwise direction, though not invariably. It is unlikely that this preliminary work on the map will produce anything like a complete answer. There will come a point at which it is necessary to go and look at the known points in the field, and to try to work out the succeeding points from the ground itself. It is a slow process, like solving a difficult cross-word, in which the various points are not necessarily identified in their logical order. It means constant interchange of method between the map and the field, testing on the map hypotheses formed in the field and vice versa.

Nor should older maps be neglected in the search for clues. The tithe maps, made in the second quarter of the nineteenth century, often show older boundaries than survive today; and the accompanying award, which gives the field-names of several generations ago, many of which have since been lost, may well produce the answer to a point or two. Estate maps, some of them going back to the seventeenth and eighteenth centuries, and a few to the late sixteenth, are also invaluable for the same reasons. Every county record office should compile a list of all the maps and plans in its own area, especially of those still in private hands, so that the searcher can know if early maps exist for his charter-country. Few have yet done so, though it would be a priceless tool for the fieldworker.

For some charters the ecclesiastical parish boundaries are a valuable clue. Frequently the charter, relating to an estate which subsequently became the core of an ecclesiastical parish, has a considerable length of common boundary with the parish. But care should be taken that comparison is made with the ecclesiastical and not the civil parish boundaries. Those shown on the current Ordnance maps are civil parishes which in many cases are somewhat different from the ancient ecclesiastical parish. Much 'tidying-up' of parish boundaries took place in the latter half of the nineteenth century, with the result that various anomalies, all of which had some historical origin and explanation, were ironed out. These 'anomalies' may well explain some point in an early land-charter. The first editions of the six-inch maps will show the older boundaries; so, too, will the tithe maps where they exist.

The elucidation of an Anglo-Saxon land charter is one of the best examples of the combination of fieldwork and documentary work for the map is, of course, a splendid historical document in itself. Once the charter is 'solved' one has the intellectual satisfaction akin to that of a mathematician who has solved a long and difficult equation.

There is little else one can do to advise about the working-out of charter boundaries except to throw the beginner in at the deep end. But it would be useful if he read beforehand a few exercises in successful solutions, both as to method and setting-out of results. See, for example, Finberg's exposition of the Hallow-Hawling charter in *Early Charters of the West Midlands* or Thomson's paper on The Early Bounds of Wanborough and

Little Hinton in the *Wiltshire Archaeological Magazine,* vol LVII. The latter paper is particularly instructive as it gives some general advice as to method and also the text of the Saxon charter, so familiarizing the student with at least the look of the original document. When the fieldworker has successfully solved a charter, or even only part of it, he will have learnt to recognize features in the depths of the countryside which are of Anglo-Saxon construction or were already there when the Old English moved in. What had previously been an ordinary ditch, for example, will be seen to be a boundary ditch of a ninth-century charter and so will acquire a greater depth of meaning; or massive hedgebanks will be found to be a boundary in a seventh-century grant, as I once found in remote and beautiful country in Devon, along a path where few people now go.

DOMESDAY BOOK AND FIELDWORK

I said in the preceding chapter that Domesday Book was a guide-book to England at the close of the eleventh century, telling us about the nature and course of human settlement at the end of six hundred years—some twenty or more human generations—of back-breaking toil. It is written in a kind of code, and once this code is deciphered the way is clear for exploration in the field. Yet it would be truer to say that it is written in a number of codes, and that the same key will not fit its text in different parts of England. Thus, to take the extreme cases, Leicestershire is primarily a countryside of nucleated villages, or was so originally, with no farmsteads between one village and the next; and Devon was primarily, but not entirely, a countryside of scattered settlement, of single farmsteads or of hamlets containing three or four farmsteads. The pattern of settlement in Norfolk and Suffolk seems different again and is equally difficult to fit into the Domesday code; yet I think it more than likely that a devoted student of the East Anglian landscape will eventually be able to tell us what Domesday is really saying about the settlement and landscape of Norfolk and Suffolk in the eleventh century. To do this, he will have to study intensively a single parish, both on the ground and on the map.

In Devon I toiled over the Domesday entry for one parish (Cadbury) until I finally discovered what it meant in terms of topography, using clues from other parishes to help in the task. The student in East Anglia would be well advised to concentrate similarly on one parish with scattered settlement today, and to wrestle with its topographical problems until he has a glimmering of what the Domesday text means. No sweeping survey of a larger area is likely to produce results that will convince one that a puzzle has been solved and that no other answer is possible. Once more I quote the words of William Blake that I have quoted elsewhere: 'To Generalize is to be an Idiot. To Particularize is the Alone Distinction of Merit.' Yet there comes a time of course when with a sufficient piling-up of close detail one is in a position to make a valid generalization. There are no short cuts in this sort of fieldwork.

Before one can engage in fieldwork arising from Domesday Book, one must have been able to identify the demesne farm (if there is one) and perhaps a number of villein farms as well. This is impossible in those parts of England where the nucleated village was the typical, and perhaps the only, form of settlement. It is impossible for two reasons: first that it is only where farmsteads are scattered about the countryside that we can identify them as distinct entities, and secondly that in the countryside of nucleated villages one also had an open-field system and this has since been swept away. So the Domesday farms, even if one could identify them at that date, have lost their original identity in the great reshuffling of lands that took place at a subsequent enclosure. No Domesday fieldwork is possible in those parts of England where the open-field system prevailed.

In the other parts of England it is possible to identify the demesne farm in a great number of cases. I have discussed a number of examples in *Provincial England*. Not all manors had a demesne farm, but most had. How does one set about identifying this farm today? First of all, it will tend to be the largest farm by far in the locality. The tithe award drawn up in the second quarter of the nineteenth century will produce this information readily enough. But occasionally a large demesne farm has been split up in later centuries, as at Sampford Courtenay in Devon (see *Provincial England,* pp. 31–2) and then it has to be pieced together from other clues.

Secondly, the demesne farm may betray itself by its name. In Western England it is frequently called *Barton.* This is an almost invariable clue. Or it may be called *Great* So-and-So. Other significant names will be Church Farm, Hall Farm, Court Farm, and *Town.* The latter name is found in Devon and Cornwall, and is used in its original Anglo-Saxon sense. Thus when we reach 'Kentisbury Town' in North Devon, as directed on neighbouring signposts, we find only the parish church and a large farmstead. This large farmstead represents the demesne farm of the eleventh century.

The next step in the inquiry is to consult the tithe map for Kentisbury parish, made in the year 1840, and to ascertain the boundaries of this farm. It is there called Kentisbury Barton, significantly enough, and amounted to 302 acres at that date. Few Devonshire farms other than old demesne farms approached this great size. Thus the identity of Kentisbury Barton with the demesne farm of 1066 is betrayed by its name, its size, and its proximity to the parish church.

Naturally the boundaries of the farm as shown on the tithe map some 750 years after Domesday may not be identical with those of the eleventh century. The determination of this point is part of the skill required by the local topographer before he goes out into the field. Where the boundary follows a lane it is likely to be original, and similarly with a stream or the edge of an old wood. If it coincides with the parish boundary it is almost certainly an original boundary of the Saxon demesne farm. A long, unbroken hedge-line, running direct across country, with other hedges butting up against it but not breaking its line, is also very likely to be an original boundary.

If neither the acreage of the farm in the nineteenth century, nor its name, present any definite clue in identifying a demesne farm, a third piece of evidence in some instances (as suggested above for Kentisbury) is the proximity of the farm to the parish church. Since a great number of English parish churches were originally founded by the local lord of the manor, and were naturally founded by him as near his own house as possible, we may look for some Saxo-Norman demesne farms in this location. Most probably, too, the church will lie to the east of the demesne farm if it is by origin a proprietary church, though this may not be an invariable rule.

Lastly there may be architectural evidence that a particular farm was the most important in its parish. It may contain medieval structural evidence that it was a house of some consequence; but this alone would not be an infallible sign.

The identification of some of the villein farms is a matter of more difficulty. If Domesday tells us that there were twelve villeins on a manor, we must generally regard this statement as meaning that there were twelve farms. The problem is to identify these beyond any reasonable doubt. There may well be more than twelve farms today. This may be the result of a splitting-up of some original farms at some time since the eleventh century, or it may be that some farms were added to the original dozen during the great colonization movement of the twelfth and thirteenth centuries. Either way there are topographical problems to be solved, akin to those arising from a Saxon land-charter. One goes on wrestling with all the evidence until everything clicks into place like a successful crossword; but like crossword puzzles one may not succeed in solving them all.

Conversely, of course, there may be fewer farms today than there were at the time of Domesday. Thus the manor of Knaptoft in south Leicestershire had in 1086 a demesne farm and twelve other farms, thirteen in all. An extent made in 1268 shows that there were then 26 farms in addition to the demesne, and an extent made in 1301 shows 24 farms besides the demesne. By the middle decades of the nineteenth century all these had been absorbed into five farms only. This remarkable diminution in the total number of farms was the result of a long and complicated history which it is impossible to summarize. But there are not a few parishes where the number of farms today is less than that of Domesday.

Nevertheless, whatever the difficulties—and these are only

43

some of them—it is possible with patience to identify at least some of the villein farms of 1086. One good general clue in separating the Saxo-Norman farms from those resulting from later colonization is that the earliest farms tended to occupy the best land. Conversations with knowledgeable local farmers should enable one to sort out the good farms from the not-so-good, and so to make some inroad into the problem of the aboriginal farms in the district.

The farms occupied by villeins in medieval times have tended to be more subject to change, in the form of amalgamations, than demesne farms. This is especially true in districts which have been dominated by large estates, on which a good deal of rationalization of farm-boundaries and throwing-together of farms may well have gone on. But a sound knowledge of the local documents and topography will enable the fieldworker to go forward with some confidence.

Further, before one can begin to identify villein farms it is necessary to know the manorial boundaries, and this is sometimes a matter of some obscurity. Manors and ecclesiastical parishes do not necessarily coincide. Some manors overlap parish boundaries; and conversely a parish may contain a number of small manors. This is frequently the case in south-western England. One cannot assume therefore that a Domesday entry relating to some manor can be equated with the bounds of the ecclesiastical parish today.

In the parish of Cadbury which was the subject of my own early inquiries there were two Domesday manors—Cadbury itself, and Bowley—and it is possible that the adjacent manor of Cadeleigh overlapped into the parish of Cadbury. The very names Cadbury and Cadeleigh betray a common origin in a personal name Cada (Cada's *burh* or earthwork, and Cada's *leah* or woodland clearing) which takes us back to a period ante-dating any manorial organization, when Cada's estate covered the greater part, if not the whole, of the two ecclesiastical parishes. Two farm-names—Kitlake and Catlake—also embody this ancient personal name. They both derive from 'Cada's stream', a boundary stream in both instances. With this sort of micro-history we are getting back to the earliest agrarian arrangements we know in this part of England. If only we could pin down Cada even to a particular century we should know a little more about the landscape-history of this small corner of Devon. We should discover, for example, the approximate date of the deep-sunken lane that now forms the boundary between the parishes of Cadbury and Stockleigh Pomeroy. It runs due north, as straight as any Devonshire lane could be expected to go, from the summit of the Raddon Hills to another summit (817 ft.) known as Windmill Hill, and thence beyond the Crediton-Tiverton road as a straight hedge-line to form the boundary between Cadbury and Cheriton Fitzpaine. Long before parish boundaries were devised, however, this lane was the artificially-made boundary between Cada's estate to the east and the large Cheriton estate to the west. It is certainly premanorial in origin, but its exact antiquity remains a matter for further research. I have no doubt that it will one day yield its secrets.

To return to the villein farms: once we are sure of their boundaries from a prolonged study of the maps, we are in a position to explore them on the ground. Discoveries on the ground may then send us back to the maps to correct what had seemed the final answer. Thus when I worked out the boundaries of Church Farm at Cadbury it seemed both from the tithe map of 1842 and the modern 2½-inch map that the western boundary was the small stream running north and south beween Higher Coombe and Church Farm. This was as near the truth as any map could show; but on the ground there was a further revelation. For a few feet *beyond* the stream, on its western side, was a conspicuous bank running parallel with the stream which was clearly the exact original boundary of the demesne farm. In other words, the stream was not the exact boundary. A pre-Conquest owner had constructed a massive bank just beyond it so as to include the whole of the stream within his own property, presumably for drinking purposes for his cattle. In this way the ground showed something which the map, not even on the largest scale, could show. I have no doubt that the exploration of the boundaries of Saxo-Norman villein farms would tell us something about early agrarian arrangements that were never recorded in any document.

It only remains to say that in 'village country' it is not possible to carry out fieldwork on this minute scale. Where the open field system prevailed, the 'boundaries' of the villein farms had no such unity as they have in anciently-enclosed country. The farms consisted of strips scattered about in two, three, or more fields; and even this identity has been lost since the enclosure of the fields into the pattern we know today. It is possible that in some open-field villages the demesne farm was a block by itself, but I doubt even so whether its early boundaries could ever be recovered. The villein farmers, certainly, lived along the village street and their farmsteads will remain for the most part unidentifiable. Many farmsteads that now stand on village streets in the Midlands undoubtedly stand on sites that were first occupied long before the Norman Conquest, and a few of these can be identified by their names. Church Farm in a Midland village is likely to be among the oldest sites in the village. And occasionally early deeds may be of considerable assistance. The Wyggeston Hospital deeds relating to the Leicestershire village of Wigston Magna go back to the late twelfth century, and it is possible to identify a few of the existing farmhouses in Bullhead Street back to *c.* 1200. In all probability their sites were occupied before the Norman Conquest, but the houses have been rebuilt many times over; and their fields today are the creation of the parliamentary enclosure award of 1767.

Even in south-western England, the existence of a village in 1066 is sufficient to complicate all Domesday fieldwork beyond much hope of success. Thus we are told of the large royal manor of Silverton in east Devon that there were 45 villeins. But we do not know the boundaries of the manor, and furthermore there was always a village and some of the ancient farmsteads must always have lain along the village street. So we do not know how many of the 45 farms to look for out in the parish and how many in the village. All the same, it is surprising what results one gets from the most intractable topographical problems if they are pursued long enough with a microscopic eye; and I feel sure that the study of Domesday topography will be immeasurably advanced within a generation or two.

3

Fieldwork in Medieval Landscapes

THE DOCUMENTARY BACKGROUND

Among the more useful records for reconstructing the medieval landscape and for initiating various forms of fieldwork are inquisitions and extents.

A neglected source for topographical inquiry lies in the *Calendars of Miscellaneous Inquisitions*, of which six volumes have so far been published covering the period 1219 to 1399. The subject indexes to these volumes give one a good idea of the kind of topographical information they contain, e.g. bridges, boundaries, parks, churches and chapels, commons and forests, mills, fishponds, vineyards, and much else. These volumes also contain many detailed extents of manors. Thus the archbishop of Canterbury's manor of Wingham (Kent) is described in the last decade of the fourteenth century as containing: 500 acres of arable land, 200 acres of pasture for the agistment of beasts, 286 acres of sheep-pasture, 12½ acres of meadow, a fishery, two water-mills and two windmills—the latter described as 'of no yearly value because they are in poor condition and ruinous'. There was also a park of 321½ acres of wood and pasture called *Gruddeswod*, a wood of 296½ acres called *Wolsech*, and 'other wood called *Biholte* of 8 acres'. Then we are told that there were twenty-five 'small buildings built in the market-place' worth 13s. 4d. per annum. Here we probably have a good example of a large market-place being partly built over with permanent stalls or shops, as happened in so many towns about this time.

The archbishop also held the barton or demesne farm of

Wingham which consisted of 140 acres of arable and 960 acres of marsh, together with a windmill 'worth nothing because the post is broken'. There are many such extents of the archbishop's lands, all full of topographical detail.

Another inquisition dated 1253 reveals the kind of houses that were built in East Street at Gloucester. They were constructed of 'boards and plaster' and covered with tiles, and contained a small hall, a chamber, and a kitchen. The site (burgage plot) was described as 33 rods long, of which 16 were built over, and 12 rods wide. Such a description is very useful for urban fieldwork and topography.

Inquiries about boundaries are numerous and of considerable value topographically. An inquisition dated 1250 leads on to a perambulation between the king's demesne lands and villein lands in the manors of Sunderland and Schoston (co. Durham), giving many landmarks as boundary-points. It refers *inter alia* to 312 acres of common pasture belonging to the manor of Sunderland which had been 'newly broken up by the men of Sunderland'.

Another inquiry made in 1243 gives detailed boundaries between the two Suffolk manors of Kersey and 'Lellesheie'; and in Leicestershire a perambulation made in 1252 gives the bounds of the 'Warren of Belvoir' (i.e. the area covered by certain hunting rights) which are full of topographical detail such as brooks, mills, sheep-folds, 'a green road', and many minor place-names.

At Whittington in Shropshire an inquiry of 1378 reveals the nature of the medieval field-system. There were, we are told, 200 acres of open land (*campestrales*) worth only 13s 4d. 'because the land is sandy and lies in common and one-third lies fallow every year.' There was also an enclosed upland pasture called 'Le Mountaynes', and four water-mills worth £8.

Nor are these inquisitions useful only for rural areas. The historian of Dunwich (Suffolk), now entirely submerged by the grey North Sea, will find valuable inquiries in the fourteenth century throwing much light on the process of destruction.

Another class of inquisition was the Inquisition Post Mortem, held on the property of landowners who held in chief (directly) from the king. These normally included an 'extent' of the properties, sometimes given in considerable detail, but the printed *Calendars of Inquisitions Post Mortem*[1] consistently fail to reproduce these 'surveys' and concentrate on the tedious minutiae of feudal tenure. There could be no better indication of the neglect of topographical research in England and of the immense bias given to these publications by the legal historians of the nineteenth century. Few students of local history realize how much material for fieldwork and exploration still lies buried in records which purport to give a full summary of their contents. It is true that medieval extents vary widely in value. Many are slight and scarcely at all informative, but others are full of detail and are essential to the local historian. They are particularly valuable where one gets a series for a particular manor, or round the time of the Black Death when many villages and landscapes underwent a drastic transformation. Thus an extent of the manor of Steeple Barton (Oxon.) taken a year or two after the first visitation of the Black Death shows that the village had been almost wiped out; and the site, in a field adjoining the old Vicarage, is now a characteristic 'lost village' site where one could pick up handfuls of broken medieval pottery.

Yet another great class of topographical record which has never (to my knowledge) been transcribed and published are the detailed perambulations of medieval forests. The late O. G. S. Crawford drew particular attention to 'the great roll of Forest Perambulations of 28 Edw. I (Pat. Roll 6A), whose national importance can hardly be questioned.'[2] The history of landscapes once covered by royal forests cannot be written unless these perambulations are examined; and there are usually several for each forest from the thirteenth century to the nineteenth. These perambulations appear to be scattered among various classes of the public records (see page 53 below).

[1] There are fourteen volumes covering the period 1235 to 1377, and three volumes covering the reign of Henry VII (1485–1509). The latter contain summaries of extents, but basically no extents are transcribed down to 1377.
[2] *Archaeology in the Field*, p. 197

MEDIEVAL PARKS AND FORESTS

Medieval parks have been studied intensively by Mr. L. M. Cantor[1] and one cannot do better than quote his words for an essential description of both parks and forests:

'The "park" was a common feature of the medieval landscape. Normally part of the demesne lands of the lord of the manor, it typically consisted of an area of woodland and pasture enclosed by an earth bank, often with an inside ditch. The bank was topped by a wooden paling fence, the whole forming an impassable barrier to the deer enclosed within the park. Occasionally the wooden paling might be replaced by a quickset hedge, or by a stone wall, and where topography made it possible, the paling fence or hedge alone might serve as an effective barrier. The enclosure was broken by gates and sometimes by "deer-leaps", specially contrived entrances which allowed deer to enter the park from the open country outside. Once within the park they were unable to get out again. The primary purpose of the park was to retain the wild animals, principally deer of the red, fallow, and roe varieties, which provided the landowner with sport and with fresh and salt meat. The park was not the only medieval hunting-ground, but differed from the others—the forest, chase, and warren—in that it was the only one that was completely and securely enclosed.

'The "forest" was a large tract of country, usually though not necessarily wooded, which belonged to the king, had its own forest laws, and came under the jurisdiction of forest officials. Within it the "beasts of the forest" (the red and fallow deer, the roe deer, and the boar) were preserved for the king's hunting. The king's forest rights were jealously guarded, and any infringement of the forest or its animals was liable, in the earlier part of the Middle Ages at least, to severe punishment.'

[1] See, for example, 'The Medieval Deer-Parks of Dorset' by L. M. Cantor and J. D. Wilson in the *Proceedings of the Dorset Natural History and Archaeological Society*, vols. 83, 84, 85 (1961-4); and L. M. Cantor, 'The Medieval Parks of South Staffordshire' in the *Transactions of the Birmingham Archaeological Society*, vol. 80 (1965). These articles also give an idea of the wide range of sources available for this aspect of fieldwork.

Medieval parks varied greatly in size. Some were small—less than a hundred acres—others were miles around. In Dorset, for example, Horn Park, which was surrounded by a fence of cleft pales of oak, contained about 70 acres, but the park at Marshwood, in the west of the county, was two or three miles in diameter. Nor are these park boundaries merely minor features in the landscape. They are, as O. G. S. Crawford says, 'among the biggest of their kind, rivalling the defensive linear earthworks like Offa's Dyke and Wansdyke, and often equal to them in size.'

A number of such hunting-parks are recorded in Domesday Book and probably date from the days of the Saxon kings. Athelstan probably hunted in the great park just outside the Saxon city of Exeter, in a rolling wooded landscape that is still called Duryard (= 'deer enclosure'), though it had ceased to be a hunting-ground before the Norman Conquest. In the whole of Devon only one park is mentioned in Domesday and that was at Winkleigh, a royal manor in the heart of the county. No obvious trace remains of this ancient park. It was 'disparked' long ago and the ground allotted to various farms on the perimeter, but I have no doubt its former boundaries could still be traced on the ground. A large area to the east of the village is to this day devoid of farmsteads and retains a good deal of woodland; and it is in this area one should start looking for the remains of a massive and continuous hedgebank that eventually completes a circle.

Very often a survey can be tracked down, complete with map, which makes the task of discovering the boundary fences of the medieval park relatively straightforward. Thus in the Devon county records is a document describing the estates of Lord Petre of Writtle. Included in this survey, made *c*. 1680, is a description of Wiscomb Park in the parish of Southleigh in East Devon. Wiscomb was an ancient hunting park of the Bonviles and was probably first made in the twelfth or thirteenth century. We are told in the survey made in Charles II's time that it was 1280 poles in circumference, which works out at exactly four miles around. It contained 640 acres, of which 23 acres were wood and streams. The streams were rich in trout, and the woods nourished raspberries, strawberries, and other wild fruits. By the time of the survey the park had been 'dis-parked' and turned into six farms. 'The hedges and ditches were made and planted in Mr. Drake's time'—so says the sur-vey. One then turns to the other Petre documents to ascertain when this was done, and a lease dated 16th November 1593 gives the answer. From this and subsequent leases it is clear that Robert Drake esquire took the park, then enclosed by 'a pale', and divided it up into farms between 1593 and 1617. So here we have a medieval boundary bank enclosing some 640 acres, and internal hedges made in the closing years of the sixteenth century. Many old hunting parks were converted into farms during the sixteenth and seventeenth centuries.

Two works should be consulted by those interested in the exploration of medieval parks on the ground today. The standard work entitled *English Deer Parks* by Evelyn Shirley (1867) contains a mass of topographical and historical informa-tion and is quite indispensable as a source. It should be stressed, however, that a great mass of information about parks still lies buried in the Public Record Office and in local record offices, not to mention muniments still in private hands. The other indispensable source, since it deals specifically with the methods and pitfalls of fieldwork, is O. G. S. Crawford's *Archaeology in the Field* (1953), in which chapter 18 deals with Medieval Castle Mounds and Parks. Crawford's pages are full of excellent practical advice which cannot be bettered.

Much the same considerations apply to fieldwork on medi-eval forests as to hunting parks. A vast amount of topographical material lies virtually untouched in the Public Record Office. Thus among the Miscellanea of the Chancery (*C.* 47) is a series of perambulations of the royal forests made in the reigns of Henry III and Edward I, with inquisitions as to boundaries. Other forest records will be found in the Special Commissions (*C.* 205) among the Chancery records. These run from 1607 to 1889. In the Exchequer records the Forest Proceedings (E. 146) contain a variety of documents from Henry III to Victoria, which include perambulations, inquisitions, and extents. There seems to be no book on English Forests comparable with

Shirley's *English Deer Parks;* but the chapter on Forestry in J. C. Cox's work *How to Write the History of a Parish* (1909) should be consulted, together with the same author's book on *Royal Forests of England* (1905). But again a vast amount of work remains to be done, probably county by county and including the fieldwork which these older writers so assiduously neglected.

MOATED HOMESTEADS

In some parts of England, above all in low-lying country of heavy clays, moated sites are numerous. They are nearly all of medieval construction and occur particularly in Eastern England and in the West Midlands. The latter may be associated with the opening up and settlement of the Forest of Arden. Similarly, the numerous sites in Suffolk and Essex are associated with the clearance of medieval woodland, particularly in the three generations between about 1250 and 1320 when pressure of population brought about the colonization of new lands.

Well over 3,500 sites have been recognized by F. V. Emery. His paper on 'Moated Settlements in England' may be found in *Geography,* vol. XLVII, pp. 378–88 and the local historian-fieldworker is referred to this for clues in documents and on the ground. Many more sites probably remain to be discovered, both from the evidence of old field-names such as 'moot' and from significant remains on the ground in the form of 'dog-leg' fragments of wet ditch, often associated with copses and difficult of access.

Sometimes a site consists of a complex of moats, as at Harlington (Beds.) where the moat surrounded the domestic buildings and another enclosed stables, cattle or sheep-pens, and a third apparently nothing but an empty enclosure.

Many sites were abandoned during the sixteenth and seventeenth centuries. But occasionally one finds a moated site still containing a house as at Old Hays, on the southern edge of Charnwood Forest in Leicestershire. Here stands a pleasant red-brick farmhouse dated 1733, surrounded by a well-kept moat.

The history of the site can be traced back to the early fourteenth century at least. Appleby Magna, in west Leicestershire, and Potter's Marston in mid-Leicestershire, are other good examples of moated sites which still contain buildings. At the latter site, the moated island was large enough to contain not only the manor-house but also a fine medieval dove-cote and a medieval chapel.[1] In Essex and Suffolk a great number of sites are still occupied by farmhouses and ancillary buildings.

These moated sites vary in size and plan. The commonest plan is rectangular, with sides of 250 ft. and 200 ft. enclosing about one acre. At the other end of the scale are such small circular moats as those in Huntingdonshire which probably protected windmills. Fuller guidance for fieldwork will be be found in Emery's important paper, and also in a classic work of a past generation, Hadrian Allcroft's *Earthwork of England* (1908) which devotes a long chapter to The Moated Homestead with many site-plans. The Ordnance Survey paper on *Field Archaeology* (1963) should also be consulted.

DESERTED VILLAGE SITES

I identified my first deserted village site in the south of Leicestershire some thirty years ago. Now they have become a familiar feature of the countryside, above all in the Midlands and East of England where the traditional settlement of nucleated villages gives rise to more or less conspicuous sites in contrast to the more obscure and smaller hamlet settlements that are characteristic of the Highland Zone of Britain.

All I remember now of the first sight of the lost village of Knaptoft was a fairly large pasture field completely filled with a regular pattern of raised platforms and narrow hollows. Such a site was baffling at the time, but it bore a resemblance to a plan shown in Hadrian Allcroft's *Earthwork of England* (p. 552) of Crow Close near Bingham in Nottinghamshire, which was identified as that of a village traditionally destroyed

---

[1] For other moated sites in Leicestershire see Hoskins, *The Heritage of Leicestershire* (1946), 13-16. Emery has recognized no fewer than 58 of these sites in this small county.

by a hurricane. It turned out that such sites had been known for years as the sites of deserted villages, but they had never been systematically written up nor related to the economic and social history of the countryside.

Having identified the nature of the site at Knaptoft, which was now clearly related to the ruined church not far away and to the large moated site to the south of the church it was possible to turn to the documents with a fresh eye. Today Knaptoft consists of only a couple of farmhouses, but in Domesday Book it contained two sokemen, ten villeins, three slaves (servi), and six cottagers (bordarii). There was also a priest, indicating that a church had existed here since Saxon times. It is unlikely that there was a resident lord as the lord was then Earl Aubrey, formerly earl of Northumbria. Assuming that the three slaves lived on the demesne farm, we have a population of nineteen households in the closing years of the eleventh century, twenty with the priest. By medieval standards this was a considerable village.

The next record to give any indication of the size of the village was an extent attached to a miscellaneous inquisition made in 1268. This begins with a capital messuage, a dovecote, and a fishpond, so there was evidently a resident lord at that date. Then there were twenty-four villeins, two free tenants, and eight cottagers. This gives a total of thirty-five households, excluding the priest.

Next come the Hundred Rolls of 1279 which state that twenty-two villeins held twenty-two virgates, and two free tenants held three virgates between them. The cottagers are not mentioned and the Hundred Rolls are therefore an incomplete record for population purposes. Another extent, made in 1301, shows that there was a capital messuage as before, and two fishponds 'within the close'. There were twenty-one villeins, two cottagers, and three free tenants. This gives a total of twenty-seven households, as against thirty-five a generation earlier.

Now follow the tax assessments of 1327 and 1332. These are even more deceptive than the Hundred Rolls as a measure of population, as they give only ten names in the former year and thirteen in the latter. About a half of the population managed to escape taxation, either on grounds of poverty or by simple evasion. The poll tax levied in 1377 lists thirty-seven names, representing perhaps a score of families, so that we may say that the village was slowly declining in size and possibly had been since the closing years of the thirteenth century.

The comprehensive tax assessment of 1524 gives two names only, that of the squire and a freeholder. But this tax, sweeping though it was, exempted some on grounds of poverty, and it is likely that a few labouring households escaped its net. Still, the fact remains that the village had virtually disappeared by the early sixteenth century; and other records suggest the appearance of large cattle and sheep pastures by the 1480s. In 1482 the squire went to law against the chaplain of Knaptoft, whom he accused of taking fifty of his steers and a hundred of his sheep. Another record dated 1507 speaks of a pasture of six hundred acres named Middle Field, which was probably the name of one of the old open fields that had been enclosed and converted to grass. So the village probably disappeared during the second half of the fifteenth century, and its site was given over to pasture like the rest of the manor. The Hearth Tax assessment of 1670 shows that there were then six houses, all on different sites from those of the medieval village.

Knaptoft was not only a well-marked site on the ground, but it turned out to have a body of documentary evidence also, which threw light on the extent of the village at its maximum and on its slow dissolution. The squire's Elizabethan Hall is now mouldering, going the same way as the old village, but most of the medieval set-up can be traced on the ground including the site of the medieval manor house (the 'capital messuage' of 1268–1301 and later) together with the fish-ponds.

There are now known to be some two thousand deserted village sites in this country. They are heavily concentrated in the Midlands and Eastern England, above all in what the geographers call the Lowland Zone. Thus in Oxfordshire there are no fewer than 101 sites which have been listed and discussed in a recent monograph.[1] In Leicestershire a provisional list names no fewer than 65 sites, some of which remain to be identified.

Local historians who wish to work upon this subject in any county are advised to get into touch with The Secretary, The Deserted Medieval Village Research Group, 67 Gloucester Crescent, London N.W.1. Lists of known sites for each county are supplied for a nominal sum, but much work remains to be done both upon the documents for each site and in the field. Almost certainly there are many sites awaiting discovery in the field in most counties, above all in the more difficult terrain of the upland counties commonly known as the Highland Zone.

The causes of the disappearance of so many English villages are various. So, too, is the chronology. Some villages probably disappeared as early as pre-Conquest times; others at the time of the Cistercian clearances in the cause of solitude. A much greater number dwindled away to nothing with the long decline of population from 1349 onwards, due to successive outbreaks of the plague. These were particularly numerous on the marginal lands which had attracted settlement in the population pressure of the thirteenth century. And many more went in the period 1450–1550 with the conversion of open fields to large pasture closes for cattle and sheep. It is a large and complicated subject and reference should be made to the writings of Maurice Beresford (especially his *Lost Villages of England*).

Many of these sites of 'lost' villages may be detected in the first instance on the one-inch Ordnance map. Suspicious signs are churches standing alone, above all where there is a moated site nearby; ruined churches, as in Norfolk particularly; large empty spaces on the map in a countryside otherwise dotted with villages at fairly regular intervals. These are particularly suspicious where a number of footpaths meet in an empty space for no apparent reason. Almost certainly they met here because there had once been a village at this point.

[1] See *The Deserted Villages of Oxfordshire* (Occasional Papers in English Local History, no. 17. University of Leicester, 1965) and *The Deserted Villages of Northamptonshire* (Occasional Papers, no. 18, 1966).

Few villages have disappeared *in toto* if only for the reason that the land must be farmed in any event. So we usually find a solitary farm or perhaps two or three scattered over a parish. At Choseley in Norfolk one farm of 666 acres now occupies the whole of the parish which was probably depopulated in the early years of the sixteenth century.

Such sites are much more difficult to detect in upland country and above all where the nucleated village was not the common type of settlement. In this kind of country one may find 'lost' hamlets at the most. These are much more difficult to detect on the map and on the ground than a whole village. They are also more difficult to find from the air. Finally their documentation presents special problems. Being hamlets and not complete parishes, they never formed separate administrative units and so were rarely the subject of separate records.

Some indication of the records available for the documentation of deserted villages has been given above in the discussion of Knaptoft. A fuller account will be found in articles by M. W. Beresford and J. G. Hurst in various local historical journals.[1] For guidance as to the appearance of deserted village sites on the ground the fieldworker is referred to *Field Archaeology* (H.M.S.O., 1963) pp. 126–8, and to chapter 4 of Maurice Beresford's *History on the Ground* (1957). Reference should also be made to the excellent air photographs and accompanying text in Beresford and St. Joseph, *Medieval England: An Aerial Survey* (1958), pp. 107–20. For some typical plans of such sites, see W. G. Hoskins, *Provincial England* (1963), ch. VI on 'Seven Deserted Village Sites in Leicestershire'.

MEDIEVAL RIVER PORTS

In medieval and later times a large proportion of inland trade went by river, far more than has ever been generally realized. Thus the major river systems—and some of the minor

---

[1] For example in Provisional List of Deserted Medieval Villages in Leicestershire (*Trans. Leicestershire Archaeological and Historical Society*, vol. xxxix, 1963–4) and Introduction to a First List of Deserted Medieval Village Sites in Berkshire (*Berkshire Archaeological Journal*, vol. 60, 1962).

ones—developed numerous little river-ports, many of them scarcely recognizable today unless one is led to them by some clue from a document. The only book on this subject covers a late period and, admirable as it is, fails to reveal the full extent of river navigation in pre-industrial England.[1]

Thus the head of navigation on the Parrett in Somerset is shown as Bridgwater in 1600–60, whereas there was a regular barge traffic as far up as Langport, and occasionally up the tributary Yeo as far as Ilchester.

In East Anglia the Yare, Bure, and Waveney were all used for navigation. Willan's map correctly shows Norwich as the head of the Yare navigation but fails to indicate that the Bure was navigable right up to Aylsham in the late sixteenth century for lighters of thirty tons and the Waveney up to Beccles for barges of twenty tons. On the Severn boats could get up as high as Welshpool, far beyond the limit of Shrewsbury shown on Willan's map. Down in Kent, the Stour is shown as navigable up to Fordwich (just below Canterbury) but sixteenth-century records show boats reaching as high up the river as Wye, at least on occasions. All along these and many other rivers were little ports which have now decayed into hamlets or single farms and betray no obvious trace of their former importance in the life of the region. Sometimes they are betrayed by their names (e.g. Hythe, which means a 'landing place'), but often the search begins with a stray reference in some medieval account roll or in a sixteenth or seventeenth century legal dispute in which the depositions may be full of topographical information.

One such old river port is Rackley, on the former course of the Axe in Somerset, about 2½ miles west of Axbridge, now a mere hamlet on a quite insignificant stream (see the O.S. 2½-inch sheet, ST 35). It has long since ceased to figure on the one-inch map. Lying under a bank of red marl, where the Cheddar Water comes nearest to the road from Axbridge, it was originally called *Radeclive* ('red cliff') and is first referred to in a Wells

---

[1] T. S. Willan, *River Navigation in England 1600–1750* (1936: new impression 1964). For the limits of navigation on the Yorkshire Ouse and its tributaries, see the map in B. F. Duckham, *Navigable Rivers of Yorkshire* (1964).

episcopal record of 1178 as *portus de Radeclive* in the parish of
Compton Episcopi. In 1189 bishop Reginald of Wells obtained
a grant from Richard I of all the lead mines on his lands in
Somerset—principally on the adjacent Mendips—and by the
same charter was allowed to make a borough and have a
market at *Radeclive*. A legal dispute in 1390 reveals that ships
docked there laden with salt, iron, fish, and other cargoes,
some of them from as far away as Darmouth and Brittany.
From Rackley, as it is now called, barges carried goods right
up to the great abbey of Glastonbury. There was indeed a
considerable system of watercourses in these northern Somerset
Levels, comparable with that round the Tone and Parrett in
the southern Levels.

An old track can be traced coming down to Rackley from the
lead-mining area by way of Callow Hill and Shute Shelve
(Gough, *Mines of Mendip,* pp. 49–50). Barges still came up-river
from Uphill and discharged cargoes of coal, slate, and salt at
the little quay in the eighteenth century. Not far from Rackley
is Hythe, now less than a hamlet, which was a similar little port.
Here the grass-covered wharves can still be seen; and there are
other small loading and unloading places. All this river trade
came to an end when floodgates were erected on the Axe at
Bleadon in 1802, so putting an end to navigation beyond this
point.

On the Parrett, in south Somerset, there are a number of
fascinating little river ports which call for fieldwork and documentary research. Combwich, on the western bank of the estuary
not far from the mouth of the river, has been a useful little port
since Roman times. Though largely superseded with the rise of
Bridgwater a few miles upstream in the twelfth and thirteenth
centuries, it nevertheless continued to ply some trade until
well into modern times. Between Combwich and Bridgwater,
on the eastern bank of the estuary, lies the now obscure hamlet
of Downend which was the riverside terminus of an ancient
route along the top of the Poldens. It was a considerable port
before the rise of Bridgwater and later, but its topography has
never been explored. Above Bridgwater we find hamlets such
as Stathe which means 'landing place', first referred to in an

episcopal record of 1233 but in all probability much older than that in origin.

The river system centred upon the Great Ouse in eastern England developed a great number of small inland ports. The Cam was navigable right up to Cambridge, but there were intermediate places such as Fen Ditton which carried on some trade. Some of these former ports now lie apparently a good way from any possible navigable water. One of these is Burwell, a large village four miles north-west of Newmarket. Roughly parallel with the main street, along which the principal houses lay, runs a channel which ultimately connected with the Cam, and running from this channel we find a series of smaller water inlets which come almost up to the back of the larger houses. These must have been little private docks for the merchants who formerly lived there.[1] The topography of Burwell would well repay a close examination, both in the documents and on the ground. So, too, would Swavesey (on the Ouse) and Outwell (on the Old Nene).

Even from this cursory discussion of the subject, it will be seen that a vast amount of fieldwork awaits the inquirer. Probably the best basis for such work is a river basin. The documentary sources are scattered and not easy to come by. Indeed, the whole subject of inland trade in pre-industrial England has been neglected for this reason, and no book has been written about it. It will have to be built up from a number of painstaking local studies for the subject is full of *minutiae* and does not lend itself to the broad sweep and the facile pen.

One should perhaps couple with the river-ports the old coastal ports that have perished completely or are represented at best today by decayed little settlements. A surprising number of small landing-places existed around our shores, above all where the coastline was full of river creeks as in Essex. Here, fortunately, we have a starting-point in official records in the Public Record Office. The need to tighten control over customable goods and the places where

---

[1] Dr. Peter Eden was the first to discover this and other 'fen stations' either along or just off the main waterways. Fen Ditton was another such 'station', and so was Isleham, which connected with the river Lark by similar cuts. I am grateful to him for these and other references.

they could be landed led to numerous inquiries in the
Elizabethan period into this problem, with the result that
there survive many lists of these minor ports and landing
places from 1565 onwards.[1] Thus under the head-port of
Kings Lynn we find listed the lesser ports and creeks of
Dersingham, Snettisham, Heacham, Hunstanton, Thorn-
ham, Walsingham, Burnham, Brancaster, Wells, Blakeney,
Wiveton, Cley, Salthouse, and Weybourne. Then follow
Sheringham, Cromer, and so round the north-east coast of
Norfolk.

What is striking about this list for north-west and north
Norfolk is the number of places which have ceased to be ports
and are now a long way from the sea. Thus Dersingham,
Snettisham, and Heacham have all been left high and dry by the
draining and embanking of the marshes in front of them.
In all these Norfolk villages there must be traces left of the
Elizabethan wharves, quays and channels which the practised
eye could decipher despite the complications of a later drainage system. Thornham now lies well inland but something of a
small decayed harbour still exists. It is possible that the medieval harbour came right up to the parish church, as it did at
Wells. Wiveton is also well inland, due to the embanking
of marshes in front of it, though in 1565 it had one ship
in the Iceland trade and a number of fishing boats attached
to it.

The inclusion of Walsingham in at least two lists (1565 and
1575) sets a problem in itself. It is difficult to believe that the
Stiffkey river was ever navigable, even for barges, as far
up as this, but the possibility certainly needs to be examined
carefully on the large-scale map and on the ground.

The basic list of ports, creeks, and landing-places compiled in 1575[2] covers the whole country and contains over 500
names, many of which will now set delightful topographical
problems. Old maps will help greatly. Thus for both Heacham
and Snettisham, mentioned above, there are maps of 1625 in
the Norfolk Record Office. There is a map of 1586 for Blake-

---

[1] The earliest are in the State Papers Domestic of Elizabeth.
[2] The P.R.O. reference is S.P. 12/135/1

ney, a map of 1649 for Salthouse, and one of 1668 for Wells-on-Sea. Other relevant maps exist for the eighteenth and early nineteenth centuries.

The worker on inland ports will find a useful guide in B. F. Duckham's article on 'Inland Waterways: Some Sources for their History', in *Amateur Historian,* vol. 6, no. 1.

GREAT YARMOUTH

One of the 156 'Rows' as it was at the beginning of this century. This unique
street-pattern was largely obliterated during the Second World War

AN OLD ENGLISH BOUNDARY

Detail of the boundary shown in Plate II showing the double hedgebank enclosing a deep lane, probably a boundary of seventh-century date

AN OLD ENGLISH BOUNDARY (Devon)

Brian Chugg

A general view of the massive hedgebank which today marks the boundary between the parish of Cadbury (*to the right*) and Stockleigh Pomeroy (*left*). This is a double hedgebank, concealing a deep and often impassable lane. It also demarcated the western boundary of the estate of one Cada (*see text*) and probably goes back to the earliest period of the Old English settlement (the second half of the seventh century in this part of England)

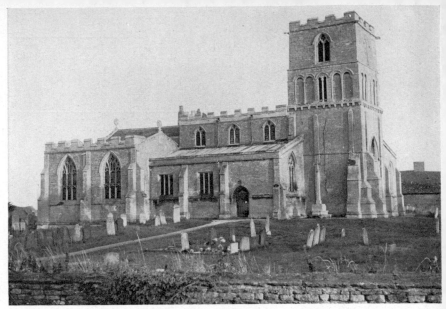

MAXEY (Northants)
An isolated Christian church probably built on a pagan burial mound

THORVERTON (Devon)
The 'Old Parsonage' built in the sixteenth century and relatively unchanged,
though now divided into three cottages

4

Towns and Villages

TOWNS

In *Local History in England* (1959) I discussed briefly the major aspects of the study of English towns. These were water-supply, other physical factors in siting, and the kinds of evidence one uses for elucidating origins and early growth. The lay-out of planned and unplanned towns was also discussed, together with some remarks on the provision of building materials by the lord anxious to get a town started on his lands. Once towns had got going, there arose the question of extensions to the original area, as instanced by such town as Kings Lynn; and at a later period we have to consider suburban growth and the 'in-filling' of an old area. I also considered briefly the formation of streets without by any means exhausting the subject.

I do not wish to go over this ground again. Some of the questions that arise in studying the topography of a town are only to be settled, if at all, by research among documents; but even so it is still necessary to walk the ground and to study what the documents are talking about. Often the first clue to the precise location of the aboriginal settlement comes from observing changes in levels which are too slight to appear on any map, however large its scale. This is true, for example, of Great Yarmouth, where much of the earliest settlement was determined by variations of level of as little as ten to twenty feet. Again, this would be true of Fenland towns such as Ely, though spot-heights on the map would tell us a good deal. Nevertheless, there are still changes of level and

65

significant alignments of streets which are best detected on the ground, and there is no substitute for this kind of physical exploration.

Before one can usefully study the growth of the street-pattern of a town one must establish where it all began. Here there have been some notable studies in recent years, to which the topographer is referred for guidance into the facts that he must take into account and the methods he should employ. Most notable of all perhaps is L. A. Burgess's *The Origins of Southampton* which is a brilliant example of how to piece together a miscellaneous assortment of topographical and other facts so as to produce a coherent pattern.[1] Then there is Frank Lee's paper on the origins and early growth of Northampton (*Archaeological Journal,* vol. CX, 1954), written in a somewhat algebraic fashion which makes for rather tiring reading. Conzen's book on Alnwick (see later) is also a study of the origins of a small town based upon a minute geographical analysis. The topographical growth of Norwich has also been studied by more than one scholar,[2] but would repay more prolonged attention, with special reference to the significance of the urban parish boundaries, as also would the interesting town of Ipswich.

The infilling of original market-places is one of the key changes in many English towns, a process which seems to have been especially active in the late thirteenth century and the early fourteenth, probably a result of the pressure of a rapidly rising population upon a limited urban space. In this process also large street-frontage tenements became divided longitudinally for the same reason. Here the inspection of old urban houses on the ground can still tell us a good deal. 'Kinks' in street-lines which cannot be explained by some obvious physical obstacle may also be detected by walking around, and may call for some radical hypothesis about obstacles which have long ago disappeared but which at the time determined the way in which streets suddenly deviated from their primary

[1] Leicester University Press, 1963. *Occasional Papers in Local History, no.* 16.
[2] An excellent recent study is *Norwich: the growth of a city* by Barbara Green and Rachel Young (Norwich Castle Museum, 1964).

direction. Here one of the facts to be taken into account may be the one-time existence of a town wall which afterwards disappeared when the burghal area was extended. I think I detect this explanation in one or two places in the street-pattern of Stamford which was once entirely walled and undoubtedly extended its burghal boundary well back in medieval times.

URBAN HOUSING

It is becoming essential to make a record of ordinary houses —working-class and middle-class—in our towns in view of the modern lust for destruction. The need to record buildings of architectural and historic importance in these circumstances is obvious enough; but the field-worker should go far beyond this elementary requirement. He should aim at producing a photographic record of every road and street built before 1914, supplying his chronology either from dated inscriptions on particular houses or from borough records; and he should try to produce photographs and plans of houses of different types from the poorest working-class house up to those of the opulent Victorian middle class.[1] I never enter a large Leicester house of this latter type, dated 1895, without wishing I could record every detail of it as a beautiful period piece. As for houses at the other end of the social scale, it is probably true to say that with the almost total clearance of slums in our towns during the past generation we may have lost information about housetypes and housing conditions which can never be recovered. It is often the commonplace which is most in need of recording. When the local historian looks back and thinks how much he would give for a street-by-street description of his village or his town in a past century, and detailed descriptions of houses of different types (if only some early chronicler had thought of the obvious at the time) he should draw the conclusion from this that it is his duty to make such a complete record for his own time, certainly for the generations down to that great watershed,

[1] For one such study in recent times, see S. D. Chapman's essay on 'Working-Class Housing in Nottingham during the Industrial Revolution' in the *Transactions of the Thoroton Society* for 1963.

the year 1914. Indeed, he may well decide also to make a sample survey on these lines down to 1939, or even the present day.

Apart from a careful noting of dated houses, with photographs and plans, derived from walking round the roads and streets, he should make a systematic search of the borough records if the council is the housing and streets authority. These records are more voluminous and varied than might be imagined.

Before borough councils as we know them achieved full control over many of their present activities such as housing and 'development' generally, a body known as the Improvement Commissioners or the Improvement Committee exercised these powers, and their records, which should survive among the borough archives today, will be a primary source for the study of street, road, and housing development. Thus at Exeter the records of the Commissioners give information about the development of streets, their maintenance, improvement and lighting. These are useful down to 1867, when the Commissioners were abolished and their powers taken over by the city council. But the council records should also be searched before 1867. They contain much information about development done independently of the Commissioners.

Thus if we may illustrate further from Exeter the kind of records that should be consulted by the student of nineteenth and early twentieth century housing, the minutes of the Streets Committee are undoubtedly the main source after 1867. From that year all applications for the construction of new buildings and for the alteration of existing ones, had to receive the approval of the Streets Committee. Here one finds information about such matters as the insertion of the bay windows so popular towards the end of the nineteenth century, or a little later the construction of garages. Dreary though the motorcar is as a subject of conversation, it has its part in social history. From the records of the Streets Committee it is possible to trace how a street began to take shape, who built the houses, with details of wall thicknesses and sanitation and kindred matters. Approval of building did not mean necessarily that the building took place at once, at least not in the year in which approval was given.

More details about the period before 1867 can be found in other records. Thus to obtain an accurate picture of the 'filling-up' of a street, the Rent Books of the Water Company are helpful. These will give an approximate date for many houses not otherwise dateable except vaguely by style (and a conservative builder can easily throw one twenty or thirty years out) bearing in mind that water was not necessarily laid on when a house was completed. These Rent Books are also valuable as a guide to the operations of builders, as they show how many houses were owned by known builders and when they were sold. They are a guide therefore to the financial operations of builders in a given town.

Far too little is known about the organization and working of the building trades, mainly because they were organized in small units which rarely kept proper business records. But the building trades were often the backbone of the smaller towns which had no special industry, and the 'building interest' on and around the town council is something one should look for. It is certainly evident enough today on many local councils, and is curiously neglected by local historians of the nineteenth century.

There are yet other records which should be consulted. The minutes of the Sanitary Committee[1] help to determine conditions in streets, courts, and tenements, and to fill in the picture given in other sources. For the earlier period the records of Turnpike Commissioners or Trustees may be useful for studying the opening up of new parts of a town by new roads on a larger scale than the ordinary builder would envisage.

It has already been stated that few local builders kept adequate records, but the records of estate agents and auctioneers are more likely to survive and may be an important source. For example, a recent collection of auctioneers' and estate agents' records for the period 1865–1965, handed over to the Wiltshire County Record Office, affords material for the detailed study of the growth of Trowbridge during this time.

---

[1] It should be borne in mind that in different boroughs, committees may bear slightly different names though they perform the same functions as elsewhere.

Local newspapers are also a valuable source. They are admittedly laborious to search. A relevant paragraph may appear suddenly amid square yards of print and may well be missed. But one may find details of when houses were built, and of ownership and rents. They sometimes supplement the bald record of the council minutes. Similarly, one should use local guides and directories for indirect evidence about urban housing and street development. Thus in Exeter the importance of the demand for artisans' houses, especially from railwaymen, can be demonstrated from the directories after about 1870.

At Leicester and doubtless in many industrial towns the records of private charitable organizations may be of the greatest help in describing the houses of the poorest element in the population. The annual reports of the Leicester Domestic Mission are of particular value in this respect.[1]

Finally, there are the large-scale maps. The Improvement Commissioners or Committee often prepared such a map at some stage in their activities. At Exeter the map made in 1840 gives the names of the larger landowners, as well as a great deal of topographical information about land about to be built on. At Leicester the medical officer of health always published maps with his annual report, perhaps merely to illustrate the incidence of particular epidemics, and these are useful as a guide to the piecemeal growth of the town from 1855 onwards.

Best of all for the detailed study of the streets and buildings in many towns are the 1:500 plans done by the Ordnance Survey between 1855 and 1895. Not all towns were covered, but a surprising number of small towns were mapped on this very large scale. A key map to the places so covered is given in *The Historian's Guide to Ordnance Survey Maps* (p. 30), a publication which should be on the shelves of every fieldworker in local history and topography. In addition to this fairly com-

---

[1] See, for example, the *Victoria History of Leicestershire,* vol. iv, on the City of Leicester, for these and other sources, esp. pp. 260 onwards. Certain records of the central government should also be consulted, e.g. the reports of the Commission on the Health of Towns, 1845. I owe most of what is said above about the Exeter council records to Dr. Robert Newton, who has used them to considerable effect in his forthcoming book on Victorian Exeter.

prehensive list of towns, a number of others were mapped on the scale of 1:528 and 1:1056 at various dates between 1843 and 1894. These too are shown on a key map in the *Historian's Guide* just mentioned. The town plans on these large scales show the layout of every building. Sometimes the various buildings on an industrial site are names according to the processes carried out therein, and the plan is therefore of immense value for industrial archaeology.[1] The various editions of the 25-inch Ordnance maps are also indispensable to the urban fieldworker. They may well show the beginnings and early stages in growth of new townships (see, for example, South Wigston in my *Midland Peasant,* p. 280: map reproduced from the 1885 edition of the 25-inch Ordnance map), and are therefore especially valuable in industrial and mining areas. The first edition of the 25-inch and 6-inch maps are now sold as 'record copies' and rightly so, as they are anything from eighty to over a hundred years old and reflect in many cases a vanished world.

URBAN STREET PATTERNS

In talking about the study of nineteenth and twentieth century housing, I have inevitably been led to some extent into the development of street and road patterns in the same period. Though they are two distinct subjects, they are often inseparable in practice since they use many types of record in common. In recent years there have been a number of studies of the physical growth of towns and suburbs, and the local historian-fieldworker will learn more from looking through these, according to the nature of his own field of interest, than from any further advice that I can give.

Thus the student of recent urban growth ought to use H. J. Dyos's *Victorian Suburb,* a brilliant pioneer study of the topographical growth of Camberwell,[2] and above all he should read and digest chapter V on The Business of Building the Suburb,

---

[1] The 1/500 plan for Stoke-upon-Trent, made in 1857, is particularly good in this respect.
[2] Leicester University Press, 1961.

both for guidance as to unusual sources and also for the treatment of the subject.

The work of J. D. Chambers on the development of Nottingham in the nineteenth century should also be referred to, chiefly *Modern Nottingham in the Making* (1945) and *A Century of Nottingham History 1851–1951* (1951). These accounts are particularly valuable for showing how the street-pattern which was developed during the second half of the nineteenth century was related to the enclosure of the town lands in 1845. For a detailed study of the growth of the neighbouring city of Leicester, the *Victoria History of Leicestershire,* vol. IV, should be consulted. In this study of an industrial town, the property boundaries of agricultural land often dictated the date and manner of 'development'. As the writer of the Leicester pages says of one particular development: 'From 1885 to 1914 piecemeal growth continued to change an agricultural landscape into one of pavement and brick. Fields and farms, and even former administrative areas sometimes retained a vestige of identity in the process by which streets were laid down in rectangular blocks to maximize the profit to be drawn from them.'

Property boundaries were important and often decisive not only in the industrial towns. Percy Russell's study of the growth of Torquay is primarily a study of the development of two large landed estates into the present pattern of mid- and late-Victorian streets and roads, and is especially valuable for the discussion of the people who actually directed these developments. At Torquay it was the solicitor to a dissolute spendthrift landowner, forced to live abroad to escape his creditors, who was mainly responsible for the urban development of the Palk estates, and who stamped Victorian Torquay indelibly with his own personality and taste.[1] On quite different lines, there is the study of Alnwick in Northumberland by the geographer M. R. G. Conzen. Conzen takes his analysis of the town-plan back to the earliest period in the history of the town, but a great deal of his study is concerned with the nineteenth

[1] See P. Russell, *A History of Torquay* (1960). The solicitor was William Kitson, who was in sole charge of the Palk estates from 1833 to 1874 (see pp. 86–90 especially.)

century and the early twentieth. He is chiefly concerned with geographical influences on a town plan and very little with the personalities behind the development; but the local topographer should take all these factors into account. Men are as important in town development as geography. One should remember the aphorism 'Cities do not grow: they are built' in order to avoid too mechanistic an approach to this side of topography. One should therefore ask continually: '*Who* planned these streets? *Who* built these houses? *Who* financed the development?' and so on.

VILLAGES

Much of what might legitimately be discussed under this heading has already been discussed in earlier chapters, or will be dealt with later—for example, farmsteads and cottages, hedges and walls, roads and lanes, fields. It only remains here to discuss the topography of the village or the parish as a whole.

There is a temptation to assume that the present site and shape of a village represent substantially the original site and shape, and that the topography of a parish—e.g. its field pattern and pattern of lanes and roads—has suffered little or no change through the centuries. In many places this may well be true, but it should never be assumed to be so. In villages and parishes which were subjected to parliamentary enclosure, or indeed enclosure at an earlier date by private agreement, it is obvious that the topography must have been radically changed at that critical date. But even in other villages a mere glance at the open spaces between the built-up plots, or at some of the 'back lanes' which are now empty, will suggest right away that many buildings have vanished from their sites and that the original village may well have had a different shape. Again, where a parish church stands alone, some hundreds of yards from the present village, one should immediately suspect that the whole village has shifted its site at some date and for some reason which requires examination. Or, again, an inspection of Domesday Book may show that the village had more families in the eleventh century than it has today. This certainly calls for further topographical exploration. What was the shape and size of the original village?

The starting-point for the exploration of village and parish topography is the first edition of the 25-inch Ordnance map. This is already an historical record, going back as it does for 80 to 110 years or so. The later revisions of these maps should also be used. There may well be important changes between the first edition and second, above all near towns or where there was marked industrial growth.

From the first edition of the Ordnance map we go backwards to the Tithe Map or the Enclosure Map, and earlier still to an Estate Map if there is one. Thus the parish of Wymondham in east Leicestershire has a large-scale estate map of 1652, showing every field, its name, acreage, and use; every road and lane; and every house and other building in the village. This can be compared in detail with the tithe map of 1844, and then with the 25-inch maps for the late nineteenth century and early twentieth. Many interesting changes are thereby brought to light. Combined with an exploration on the ground, this gives us a period of more than three hundred years of topographical change.

The oldest estate maps, on a scale suitable for this kind of fieldwork, date from the last quarter of the sixteenth century, but they are not common. In Norfolk, for example, there are several maps for this period in the Holkham Estate Office (e.g. West Lexham, 1575) and the Norfolk Record Office contains many others. Some villages have a remarkable series (e.g. Flitcham from 1550–80 onwards). For Kent the estate maps begin in 1589, the oldest maps being those of estates belonging to All Souls College, Oxford, and still housed in the library there. It is clear that where there are large landowners like the Cokes of Holkham, or college estates, the chances of finding early maps are vastly increased. In some counties (e.g. Devon) even seventeenth-century maps are not plentiful.

Villages which underwent parliamentary enclosure in the latter part of the eighteenth century or the early nineteenth may well have large-scale maps showing 'before' and 'after'. The earlier map should show the village and its farmsteads and cottages, and outside it the complete lay-out of the open arable fields, the commons (if any), roads, lanes, and bridle-paths, and every other topographical detail. The later map will show the new 'allotments' made by the enclosure com-missioners, but probably not all the hedgerows (the internal hedgerows of each allotment were made later).[1] It will also show the new roads of the parish, laid out by the commis-sioners, and the untouched homesteads and 'ancient closes'. One of the topographical problems in this kind of country is to find out what effect this large-scale enclosure had upon the village itself. Sometimes farmers immediately built themselves a new house out in the fields where none had been before. Thus the Leicestershire parish of Sileby was enclosed in the year 1760, and the one-inch map shows Hanover Farm, Belle Isle, and Quebec House, all out in the newly-created fields. It needs no exploration on foot to decide when these farmsteads were built. But in many parishes the effect of enclosure on the shape of the village, and the settlement of the parish, was long delayed—perhaps until Victorian times. Enclosure was a costly business and not all farmers could afford to build a new house out in the middle of their new lands: this had to wait for a generation or two. It is usually very difficult and sometimes impossible to trace this process from documents, and an exploration on foot of every farmhouse out in the fields is the quickest and surest way of settling this problem.

In those parts of the country not affected by the enclosure movement, where the pattern of settlement has always been that of scattered farmsteads or hamlets surrounded by their own small fields, the continuity of the topographical pattern is much less likely to have been seriously disturbed. This is certainly true in Devon, about which I have written a good deal in one place and another, though whether it is so true on the estates of the large landlords I do not know. It is possible that they made considerable changes in the arrangement of their farms in the interests of rationalized farming in the eighteenth and nineteenth centuries and that farms have changed their

[1] See my *Making of the English Landscape* (1955), esp. pp. 153–4, and *Leicester-shire: the History of the Landscape,* pp. 90–94.

immemorial identity. On the other hand, the convoluted physical topography of the Devon landscape, and the existence of thousands of miles of massive hedgebanks dating from a much earlier period of time, made it difficult even for the larger landlords to effect much radical change here. In south-eastern England, some parts of Kent at least show the same remarkable stability. As Dr. Alan Baker has said recently in 'Some Fields and Farms of Medieval Kent': 'The origins of the present rural landscape are to be sought beyond 1600 . . . Kentish rural settlement and field patterns were already by the beginning of the fourteenth century established in a form which has remained basically unchanged to the present day.'[1]

One could certainly say the same of most of south-western England and of considerable parts of Hertfordshire, to mention only a few regions out of many where this continuity could be traced by the assiduous topographer prepared to use documents and to explore the ground itself.

---

[1] In *Archaeolgia Cantiana,* vol. LXXX (1965), pp. 152–74. See also his article on 'Some early Kentish estate maps and a note on their portrayal of field boundaries' in *Arch. Cant.,* vol. LXXVII (1962), pp. 177–84, and 'Field Patterns in seventeenth-century Kent' in *Geography,* vol. 59, (1965), pp. 18–30. Dr. Baker's work upon Kent settlement and landscapes is a model for other geographers and should be read carefully by all local historians interested in this aspect of fieldwork. Another brilliant study, also by a geographer, is *The Lord and the Landscape* by Professor Harry Thorpe (1964). It deals with the parish of Wormleighton in Warwickshire from its origins to the present day as a study in the evolution of a landscape.

5

Place-Names and Topography

All place-names have a meaning, and a great number of them tell us something special about the early history of a place. Few names are totally uninformative. Many offer useful clues for further fieldwork if used with a little imagination. A high proportion of place-names (including names of farms where they are ancient) include a topographical element, and topography implies exploration in the field.

Those working on place-names are strongly advised to use Ekwall's *Dictionary of English Place-Names* as their bible, or the appropriate county volume of the English Place-Name Society where it has been published. Certain counties (e.g. Kent, Dorset, and Lancashire) have their own scholarly volumes published independently of the Society, all edited by Swedish scholars. In no field is guesswork so dangerous as that of place-names. The expert is not invariably right, but one should have a good reason for differing from him in the interpretation of a name.

Nevertheless, the local historian should be warned that Ekwall and his Swedish followers, and the English Place-Name Society generally, seem to me to be much stronger on English names than they are on Romano-British. There are probably more place-names deriving from Celtic origins than we yet suppose. I believe myself that there was a much greater degree of continuity of life from Roman Britain into Old English times than is usually allowed, and some of this may be reflected in the place-names of a district. On this subject I have delivered the 1966 O'Donnell Lecture in the University of Edinburgh, entitled 'Maps and Landscapes: a Contribution to the Problem of Continuity', which I hope to publish in the not too distant future. It is noteworthy, too, that the English Place-Name Society have not published any substantially 'Celtic' volume of place-names (e.g. Cornwall, prepared long ago but still not published). The student of place-names, and the local historian generally, are greatly hindered by this Teutonic over-emphasis in the field of place-names as in other historical fields. Yet, for all this critical note, the amateur should still proceed carefully in assessing the significance of place-names in his chosen territory, and confine himself to the available evidence.

Even if one has an authoritative interpretation of a name, its bearing upon the early history and topography of a place may still be ambiguous. Thus the Cotswold village of Bibury derives its name from Beage's *burh* or fortified place, and Beage can be identified as the daughter of one Earl Leppa. Leppa and Beage received this estate from the bishop of Worcester early in the eighth century. It must have had an earlier name (now lost) which was changed when Beage took it over and in all probability made it her residence. In explaining the place-name, therefore, as 'Beage's *burh*', we are a long way from having arrived at the ultimate origins of the village. When did the bishop of Worcester or his predecessors receive this estate, and from whom?

The boundaries of this estate, as granted some time between 718 and 745, have been worked out by G. B. Grundy (see 'Saxon Charters and Field-Names of Gloucestershire', in the *Transactions of the Bristol and Gloucestershire Archaeological Society*, 1935–6, pp. 40–3) but anyone working on the early history of Bibury or its neighbourhood should walk these boundaries and check them against the wording of the grant. Grundy worked overmuch in studies or in libraries, and rarely worked out his boundaries in the field. He needs checking (like most of us). Incidentally, another Saxon charter—a grant of land by a later bishop of Worcester relating to Ablington on the Coln— reveals that a church existed at Bibury as early as the year 899. The grant reserves church-scot and soul-scot to *Beganbyrg,* which must have been the mother-church. Already, then, we have accumulated a number of topographical facts about the the early history of Bibury and raised questions which call for fieldwork. One last question: Bibury is clearly an ancient estate, already a going concern in the early eighth century with a history of unknown length before that: what is its relationship, if any, to neighbouring Roman villas and their estates?[1]

It is possible that a considerable number of places changed their names, as Bibury did, with a change of ownership. Sometimes there is direct documentary evidence for this change of name. In other cases it is a matter of simple deduction. Thus the large village of Wigston Magna in mid-Leicestershire has a Scandinavian name meaning 'Viking's *tun*', a name derived from a Danish personal name and not likely to have been given before the Scandinavian conquest of Mercia in the year 876. But, just outside the village, a large Anglian cemetery of pagan date (sixth-seventh century) was found many years ago. This clearly served the original Old English village at that time, and this village must have had an older name than Viking's *tun*. This original name is now completely lost, but the history of the village is established as some three hundred years older than its present name would imply. There are many other villages within the Danelaw to which these remarks would apply.

PLACE-NAMES ON THE NORFOLK COAST

After these general warnings about the pitfalls in the use of place-names as evidence, let us consider some examples of what can be deduced from the intelligent use of such names, and the kind of questions they give rise to. For this purpose we can take a short stretch of the Norfolk coast between Yarmouth and Cromer, and take every village-name in turn. Some will tell us little from a topographical standpoint, but few are without some value as pointers to fieldwork. Immediately to the north of Yarmouth is Caister, a simple example meaning 'a camp', and

---

[1] At Withington, some eight miles higher up the Coln valley from Bibury, Professor H. P. R. Finberg demonstrated with a high degree of plausibility a continuity between the Romano-British estate associated with a villa and the Anglo-Saxon estate which succeeded it. See 'Roman and Saxon Withington' in *Lucerna*, pp. 21–65.

usually Roman in this context. Here a small Roman town, first settled about A.D. 125, has been excavated in recent years on the higher ground to the west of the parish church. This town fell into ruin with the collapse of the Roman administration in the early fifth century, but about A.D. 650 an Anglo-Saxon village was established in and around the ruins. Thus Caister, a fairly obvious place-name, has begun to yield its secrets; but here it is more a matter for the pure archaeologist than the local historian-fieldworker.

Immediately beyond Caister, however, we come to a group of Danish village-names ending in *-by*. These are Scratby, Ormesby, and Hemsby, all derived from Danish personal names. Scratby seems to be a 'lost village'. It is merely a name on the map and the parish has now been absorbed into Ormesby St. Margaret. Somewhere on the southern edge of Ormesby St. Margaret, then, there may be a village site awaiting identification.

But the thick and highly localized cluster of Danish place-names in this piece of country raises topographical problems. Are we to assume that this fertile district was empty of English settlers when the Danes arrived in the year 879? There are Old English names on all three sides (the sea is on the fourth) so why should this piece of country, about seven miles by four, have been left unoccupied? I suspect that the Danes took over a number of villages in this area and gave their personal names to them. But if the existence of an earlier settlement is to be demonstrated conclusively the evidence will have to be archaeological, as at Wigston Magna in Leicestershire.

Mr. Charles Green[1] does not believe that there was any settlement in this district known as Flegg, to the north of Yarmouth, before the Danish soldiers arrived in the year 879. In that year, the Anglo-Saxon Chronicle records, 'the host went from Cirencester into East Anglia, and occupied that land and shared it out'. Mr. Green regards them as merely taking over an empty countryside, so far as Flegg and other local areas were concerned. Certainly no pagan cemeteries have been found in

[1] In letters to the author and in articles in the *Eastern Daily Press* for August 18, 19, 1965.

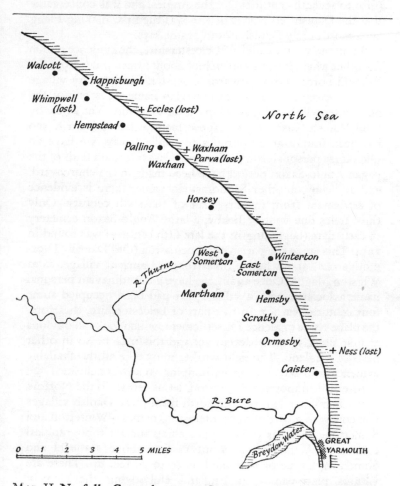

MAP II **Norfolk Coast between Cromer and Great Yarmouth**
(Showing all places mentioned in the text). Note that there
are no fewer than four 'lost villages' in this small piece of
country.

Flegg to suggest that there had been an earlier settlement (fifth to seventh centuries) by the Angles, and it is conceivable that the Danish settlement of 879 was the first, making Flegg 'an almost purely Danish island', as he says.

But in the Wreak valley of Leicestershire, the evidence points the other way. Here, in a stretch of about fifteen miles from the Rutland border down towards Leicester, nearly every village without exception has a Scandinavian name. It is one of the most intensely Scandinavian parts of England. Yet at Saxby (Old Danish 'Saxi's *by*) a large cemetery dating from *c.* 500 has been found; at Sysonby, a few miles away, we have an Old Norse personal name—Sigstein's *by*—but again finds of the pagan Anglo-Saxon period have been made in the churchyard; and at Beeby, another Scandinavian name, there is evidence of settlement from the first half of the sixth century. Only three miles due west of Beeby, a large Anglo-Saxon cemetery of early date (beginning in the late fifth century) was found in 1954. This lay in the parish of Thurmaston (Old Danish 'Thormoth's *tun*') about half a mile from the ancient village, as at Wigston Magna. Once again, we have a Scandinavian personal name associated with a village that had been occupied some four centuries earlier. In this part of Leicestershire, therefore, the place-name evidence for settlement, which looks so obvious at first sight, is quite deceptive; and this may be so in other parts of England. The field-worker must take all the available evidence into account before jumping to any conclusion.

After this important digression, let us return to the Norfolk coast. A mile or two farther north from these Danish villages one comes to a pair of very interesting names—Winterton and Somerton. Obviously these have some ancient topographical connexion. Winterton is about 12 feet above sea-level and Somerton, a mile or so inland, is 30 to 40 feet up. There are various place-names in England embodying the element 'summer', usually referring to the movement of flocks and herds to summer pastures (e.g. Somerton in North Oxfordshire and Somercotes in the Lincolnshire marshland). Here in Norfolk the position seems to be reversed. Winterton is on the lower ground and is, moreover, exposed in winter to bitter winds from the sea. But clearly Somerton and Winterton, so near together, were connected in some way in pre-conquest times. The way the parish boundaries run also reveals that the two parishes originally formed a single estate. How do we explain this?

Somerton was probably the parent village, a 'normal' agricultural settlement. The move to winter quarters was for the purpose of catching the larger codling which move inshore as the colder weather sets in. This source of food, in a primitive economy, was too valuable to ignore. Line-fishing from small boats was the method practised. Huts provided the winter quarters in the first place, probably more like a camp than a regular settlement, and only occupied in the autumn and winter months. But as time went by this temporary camp developed into a permanent settlement, certainly by the time of Domesday Book. Hence the name 'Winterton', reflecting a farmer-fisherman economy of Anglo-Saxon times.

Somerton itself takes the form of two distinct settlements—East Somerton and West Somerton—barely half a mile apart. It has been suggested by Mr. Charles Green that East Somerton, where the parish church is now in ruins, was the parent settlement, and that West Somerton had its origin in another temporary camp, this time a summer camp, for the digging of the brushwood peat in the west of the parish. Martham Broad represents the flooded peat-diggings of this period and later, down to medieval times. The eastern side of this Broad is scraped clean of its peat down to its gravelly margin.[1]

It is possible that Somerton itself was a comparatively late settlement from an older village farther inland. Such 'summer' names are usually secondary in date. If so, then the large village of Martham might have been the earliest settlement (though its name is quite unrevealing) as the expansion of settlement almost certainly took place from an aboriginal inland village towards the marshes and the sea. But it is at any rate clear that these two place-names—Somerton and Winterton—open up a wide range of discussion of topographical problems in this small area.

Going northwards again, we come to Horsey. This, too is a

[1] Charles Green, article in *Eastern Daily Press*, 2nd August 1963.

revealing name: it means 'horse island'. It must have been an island of upland in the fen, a mile or so in diameter, on which feral horses grazed in Saxon times, so giving the island its distinctive name when the first settlers moved in. These feral horses were strictly wild mares, referred to in Domesday Book as *equae sylvaticae* at various places in Norfolk. Herds of from 12 to 36 are mentioned in several parishes in Norfolk. At Hockham in the south-west of the county there had been a herd of 220 wild mares in Edward the Confessor's time, but none remained by 1086. Similarly none are recorded at Horsey in 1066–86. They had probably disappeared long before when the island was taken over and broken up for permanent farming. But at Palling, only three miles along the coast, fourteen wild mares still survived in 1086.

Next along the coast comes Waxham, which could mean 'watchstone *ham*'; but it is probably useless to look for the site of the watchstone as part of the original pre-conquest estate (Waxham Parva) is now under the sea. That such a watch was kept is highly likely as this is a most exposed and dangerous coast. Palling next along the coast has today both a coastguard station and a lifeboat station. It is possible that the road (B. 1159) running from West Somerton to Palling, on which Waxham stands, represents the line of an old seabank. Its frequent abrupt bends would suggest this. If so, the watch-stone may have been roughly where Waxham church now stands, near an acute bend in the bank.

Of the name Palling little need be said except that it means 'Paelli's people'. It is one of those names ending in *-ingas* which denotes a settlement of the earliest period in Anglo-Saxon times, probably in the fifth century. It would have been one of the first landfalls to be made by the migrants from the northwest shores of Europe. Within a couple of miles are a couple of other early settlements of the same period—Hickling and Lessingham.

Rather more than a mile along the coast again is the lost village of Eccles, now not even a name on the map but marked only by the words 'St. Mary's church' in Gothic type; and all that is left of the church is a confused heap of stones on the

84

beach at low tide. Eccles is the British word for 'church'. Here there must have stood a very early Christian church indeed, one of the first in Norfolk, perhaps dating from late Roman times, and possibly an indication that British survivors were to be found here when the earliest Anglo-Saxons moved in. The name Eccles occurs in other parts of England and is so interesting that it is discussed separately below. As to the possibility of British survivors on this coast, so open to invaders, we have additional evidence in another place-name—Walcott—only four miles away. This means the 'cottages of the Welsh or *Wealas*'. *Wealas* was the general name given by the Anglo-Saxons to the British they encountered in various parts of the country. That some pockets of British survived into Anglo-Saxon times, and were left alone so long as they gave no trouble, is well attested elsewhere.

Last in this brief topographical excursion is the name Happisburgh. This, too, must have been one of the earliest settlements in this part of Norfolk. The name derives from 'Haep's *burg*', *burg* or *burh* being a fortified place or a fort. This fortified place possibly lay on the knoll rising to well over 50 feet above sea-level and now crowned by Happisburgh church; or could it have been one of the lost forts of the Saxon shore? 'Haep's people' gave their name to Happing hundred, now an area of some twenty-seven thousand acres which perhaps represents their original territory. Haep himself occupied the stronghold now represented by Happisburgh.

PLACE-NAMES AND ANCIENT CHURCHES

A number of place-names, scattered around England, embody the British word *ecles* (*eglos* in Cornwall, *eglwys* in Wales) meaning 'a church'. This generally, if not invariably, refers to a pre-English church and is therefore of considerable interest topographically.

The Eccles referred to above can tell us little, for it was finally destroyed by the sea in the seventeenth century; but there is another Eccles in Norfolk, about a mile or so off the Norwich-Thetford road, in a countryside with much heath and common. The parish boundary tells us little of its past history as a church; for whatever British church existed here perished in all probability long before parochial boundaries were established. A Roman road passes within half a mile of the present Eccles church, and just off this road lies the early settlement of Harling. A considerable number of roads still meet at Eccles, though the village has practically disappeared and the landscape has been modified by an airfield and modern forestry planting. One would expect a considerable Roman-British settlement, or perhaps a large Roman villa, to turn up somewhere round here eventually.

Between six and seven miles south-west of Eccles is other important evidence of Romano-British survival in these parts. This is the now minute settlement of Brettenham, on the north bank of the river Thet. It means 'Bretta's ham'. A mile to the north-east of the present village a Romano-British settlement has been found, just where a Roman road crosses the Thet, dating from the latter part of the first century. Similarly, on Micklemoor Hill, just north of West Harling church, an Iron Age farmstead has been found. All this is not far from Eccles: so far as any place-name offers a clue to a buried site this is a likely place for a major discovery.

There is an Eccles in Kent, about a mile north of the ancient settlement of Aylesford and today quite an insignificant name on the map. Eccles is now in the parish of Aylesford; it has lost its identity as an ecclesiastical site. Recently 'a villa of exceptional size and early date' has been excavated.[1] The occupation of this villa dates at least from the Claudian period, and probably earlier. It was possibly the house and estate of a native nobleman 'seeking to copy the Roman way of life shortly after the Conquest.' Christianity had reached Britain by the second century and spread steadily in the third and fourth centuries. An important villa such as that now being excavated at Eccles would have acquired a church during this period, a building which perhaps survived the villa and was known to the first Anglo-Saxon invaders.

At Widford, on the western edge of Oxfordshire, the little

[1] See *The Times* for 23 September 1964.

church of St. Oswald was built right over the tessellated pavement of a Roman villa. This was almost certainly no accidental choice.

A number of Lancashire place-names embody the element *ecles*. Eccles takes its name from the church of St. Mary in Barton-upon-Irwell. Barton itself indicates a past importance, for it means 'demesne farm', probably the demesne farm of the royal manor of Salford. St. Mary's church at Barton probably stands on the site of a British church.

Other Lancashire places with the same history are Eccleshill and Eccleston. There is no trace of a church at Eccleshill today. As for Great Eccleston, it is now part of the parish of St. Michael-on-Wyre which had a church in 1086 when it was known as *Michelescherche*. Here there seems to have been a break in the continuity of the church-site, and it remains for the local historian-fieldworker to establish what is likely to have happened.

Eccleshall in Staffordshire retains some of its ancient importance. In the middle of the nineteenth century it was described as one of the largest and most fertile parishes in the county, covering upwards of 20,000 acres of land and including twenty-one townships or liberties. Beyond doubt it was a centre of Christian worship in Romano-British times. There is a tradition that a temple of Jove was built here by the Romans and afterwards consecrated as a Christian church. Tradition by itself is almost valueless, but it sometimes affords a clue to the historian that should not lightly be cast away. St. Chad resided here in the seventh century, and the bishops of Lichfield had their seat here for many centuries. There is no doubt about the antiquity of Eccleshall as a place, but much remains for the active field-worker to elucidate. The enormous size of the parish suggests an aboriginal estate that remained undivided until recent times; but even more directly significant is the place-name Walton. This is the name of a township on the great estate of the bishop. It means 'Welshmen's village' and is clear evidence that a native British settlement still survived here when the Saxons moved in some time in the seventh century.

There are other place-names which throw light upon the history of settlement by indicating beyond doubt that certain churches existed at an early date. *Minster* names are especially important in this connection. The original meaning was the general one of 'monastery' or 'a large church served by secular clergy', often with the special meaning of a mother-church which served a large area around it by means of missionary-priests. From the work of these early missionaries daughter-churches were founded in outlying settlements. The mother-church almost certainly stood in the mother-village; hence the *minster* name tells us about the course of settlement of a particular district. Such a name is Leominster in Herefordshire, which was the minster for a district anciently known as *Leon* around the rivers Arrow and Lugg. Leominster was the first church built by the reigning family of this region, probably about the middle of the seventh century, though one story has it that it was founded by St. David, whose arm-bone was still treasured by the church in the thirteenth century.

Often a mother-church does not reveal itself by its name but through some other record. Thus the Matriculus of Bishop Hugh Welles of Lincoln (early thirteenth century in date) shows that Market Bosworth in west Leicestershire was the mother-church of four surrounding villages and their churches. Similarly, Melton Mowbray in north-east Leicestershire was the centre of a group of five daughter-villages.

The name Stow, either by itself or compounded with another word, usually indicates a church of ancient foundation, going back to the missionary days of Christianity. It means 'a holy place, a place of assembly'. The element 'church' or 'kirk' obviously denotes an early church. Sometimes the name of the founder is incorporated in the place-name: thus we get Alve-church in Worcestershire, which is 'Aelfgyth's church', and Offchurch in Warwickshire which is 'Offa's church'; and Honey-church in Devon ('Huna's church') to name only a few. Probably these churches, built by private landowners, go back to about the tenth century, when proprietary churches were being founded in some numbers. Pucklechurch in Gloucestershire means 'Pucela's church' and is first recorded in 946, though it

88

may of course have existed for some time before it is named in any surviving record.

Another place-name which indicates the existence of an early church is Cheriton. There are Cheritons in Devon and Somerset, Hampshire and Kent; a Churton in Cheshire and Chirton in Wiltshire, all with the same meaning. Many 'church' names are compounded with the names of their dedication-saints. These are usually less informative than names which include the name of a secular founder, though unusual dedications (such as St. Pega at Peakirk in Northamptonshire) may be very helpful in establishing the chronology of a site.

OLD AND NEW

A great number of place-names embody the element 'old' or 'new'. These names tell us something of the history of the place, though precisely what they are saying may not be immediately apparent. It may well require a visit to the site, and some field-work around it, before one can be certain of having extracted the full significance of the name.

'New' and 'old' in place-names have no absolute age: they are 'new' or 'old' in relation to each other, or to some other place. In fact, one could well ask: how old is new?

There are many 'new' places recorded in the eleventh century, some even earlier. Newtimber in Sussex is so called in 960, Newbald in the East Riding in 963. The New Forest is so called in Domesday Book; and there are scores of villages called Newton at the same date. Newark in Nottinghamshire is 'the new work' in 1054–7, probably a fortification erected in the Anglo-Danish wars (between 878 and 915) and so called to distinguish it from the ruined Roman towns of *Ad Pontem* (Thorpe by Newark) and *Margidunum* (East Bridgford).

Newbury, in Berkshire, first recorded about 1080, is a similar name. The various 'Newports' recorded in the eleventh century are of special interest. New *port* is the 'new market-town'. Among these are Newport Pagnell, Newport in Essex, and Newport in Shropshire.

The last-named illustrates one of the pitfalls of Domesday Book and place-names. It is not mentioned in Domesday Book but occurs for the first time in a record in 1174 as *Novus Burgus*. Nevertheless, this reference by itself is deceptive, for the town was already over a hundred years old. Its name occurs on a coin of about 1050 as *Niweport;* but in Domesday Book it is silently included in its parent manor of Edgmond, to the west. In investigating the origins of towns, the evidence of coins should not be forgotten. Both Totnes (Devon) and Langport (Somerset) are first evidenced in coins, long before they appear in written records. So, too, is Bristol.

Many names embodying 'new' are comparatively late in date, as we should expect. They range from the twelfth century to the fifteenth century and later. Thus the town of Newmarket appears as *Novum Forum* in the year 1200, a new market-town astride the great road from London to Norwich. Its late origin is revealed by the fact that it lies in two different counties. The mother-village was Exning, about two miles away. It is said that the market was moved from Exning on account of plague there, but more probably the town grew up naturally along a busy medieval road, like so many towns of comparatively late origin.

Various places called Newland all seem to date from the thirteenth century, when the clearance of new land was at its height. In all these cases we must look for the parental village from which this colonization took place.

Names embodying 'old' are equally provocative for topographical fieldwork; though once again there are pitfalls. Thus the village of Old in Northamptonshire derives its name from *Wald,* 'a wood', and Oldbarrow in Warwickshire is 'Ulla's barrow'. Oldcoates in Nottinghamshire means 'cottages inhabited by owls'.

But names like Old Buckenham, Old Romney, Old Sarum, and many others, when there is a 'New' not far away, mean what they say. Old Buckenham (Norfolk) is now a rather dispersed village, with the remains of a small twelfth-century castle. A new castle, on the road from Bury St. Edmunds to Norwich, was built on heath-land in the latter part of the twelfth century. New Buckenham grew up as a small, planned town some 200 yards from the new castle, and by the early fourteenth century was richer than the mother-village.

The relationship of Old Sarum and New Sarum (Salisbury) is well known, but the precise relationship between Old and New Romney still remains to be worked out. New Romney seems to have grown up (like Great Yarmouth) on a sandbank, and its street-pattern, like Yarmouth again, has been determined by this basic topographical fact. Wherever we find the element 'old', then, in a place-name, we have some topographical problems to solve.

A number of towns have a district called Old Town. Such a town is Brackley (Northamptonshire) where the one-inch map marks 'Old Town' well outside the present urban area. Here, too, is the ancient parish church of St. Peter, a twelfth-thirteenth century building well away from the present town. 'Old Town' represents the original site of the village of Brackley. When a borough was laid out along the main road from Oxford to Northampton early in the thirteenth century, the village-site was more or less abandoned. Hence the present apparent isolation of the parish church. Even the 'Old Town' was a secondary settlement, made in or before the eleventh century, from the now-minute settlement of Halse 2½ miles away. The parish of Brackley St. Peter was carved out of the original Saxon parish of Halse. (See Beresford and St. Joseph, *Medieval England: an Aerial Survey* (1958), p. 209.)

Exactly the same thing happened at Chard (Somerset) and Honiton (Devon), both towns of essentially one long street—the ancient road to the south-west from London, now the A.30. At Chard there is a part of the town, well away up the hill, called Old Chard. Here one finds the parish church. When the lord of the manor, the Bishop of Bath and Wells, set up a borough at Chard in the year 1235, he laid it out along the busy main road half a mile away, and just as at Brackley the church was left within a dwindling farming community. At Honiton there is no part called Old Honiton but the parish church stands nearly a mile outside the town, well up the hill-side where the original Saxon village lay. Here a town grew up along the main road in the closing years of the twelfth century, and the parental village was completely abandoned.

Other examples of Old and New are Alresford (Hampshire) and Woodstock (Oxfordshire). At Barnsley (Yorkshire) there is an Old Town; and in Surrey we find Old Woking which represents the original ancient village before the centre of gravity moved to the new railway-line. When the London & South-Western Railway was opened in 1838 'the station was placed in the midst of an open heath, and for many years a public-house (the *Railway Hotel*) was almost the only dwelling near it. Since then many places of business have grown up near the Station, and a number of good residences have been built on Maybury Common. . . .' So says Murray's *Handbook for Travellers in Surrey* (1898 edition). Murray's Handbooks are an invaluable storehouse of topographical information for the British Isles in the second half of the nineteenth century.

Scattered over the map of England there are countless examples of 'Old' and 'New' in place-names. Where they occur in close conjunction to each other, they present an immediate topographical problem. Even the word 'old' by itself is worth further inquiry. What for example is the precise significance of Oldland in Gloucestershire, which was so called as long ago as Domesday Book? Here is a good problem for the local field-worker. Or there is Yelland, which occurs several times in Devon, with the same meaning. To what distant period does 'old' refer in these instances?

OTHER NAMES

All names embodying 'summer' and 'winter' are worth special examination. I have discussed some of these elsewhere. For example, I discussed the precise topographical significance of Somerton in the Cherwell Valley (Oxfordshire) in *Local History in England* (1959), p. 44. Somercotes, in the Lincolnshire marshland, is discussed in *The Making of the English Landscape* (1955), p. 64. One other place-name element deserves comment. This is 'black', especially as in Blacklands. Long-continued human occupation of one site produces a marked darkening of the soil, either by the accumulated household wastes or by the burning of a building. On many of these sites excavation has produced evidence of Roman occupation. The name Blacklands occurs no fewer than fourteen times in the field-names of Oxfordshire. All these call for investigation by competent field-workers. In Devon, too, there are at least four old farms called Blackland or Blacklands, all so called in medieval times and thus reflecting human occupation of even greater antiquity. In the south of England the field-name 'Chessels' 'has proved time and again to mark a Roman villa site', (see *Field Archaeology* (H.M.S.O. 1963), pp. 9–10), probably arising from the ploughed-up remains of building-stone, tiles, and tesserae from mosaic pavements buried underground. In the depths of north-west Norfolk is the parish of Choseley, formerly a village with a church but now consisting only of one farm. The name means 'the gravelly clearing', from the Old English word *ceosol*. The soil here is naturally gravelly, but there may well have been a Roman villa here, still awaiting discovery; in 1942 a Roman coin hoard was unearthed here. It is only a matter of time before the villa itself is located.

I have myself found a Roman villa at Hamilton in Leicestershire (while looking for something entirely different) by observing a large, whitish patch in the middle of a grass-field which had just been cut across to make a land-drain. On closer examination, the patch consisted of a large scattering of tesserae, composed of white limestone, where the excavator had broken through a buried villa-floor. Such 'gravelly' traces of buried villas must have been not uncommon in Anglo-Saxon England and would have naturally given rise to a special field-name or even a place-name.

6

Small Houses

The systematic study of the houses of a parish, a town, or a region, will tell us a great deal that is nowhere recorded in documents. Yet few local historians have attempted this task, partly because they are still blind to the high value of visual evidence and partly because, if they are aware of the existence of this evidence, they feel it is beyond their powers and knowledge. This need not be so.

Houses may be studied purely as structures by those who are interested in the techniques and materials of the building trades, with particular reference to timber-framed houses. Yet this is only half the story. We ought to place all types of houses in their human background and relate them to the social and economic history of their immediate surroundings. Without this framework and background we only dimly understand what we are looking at. One has often accused historians of ignoring the value of visual evidence; but the students of vernacular building, in their zeal for peg-holes, types of roof-trusses, straight joints and so forth, remain woefully ignorant of the documentary side of their field of study and seem to be as indifferent to it as the historians are to fieldwork.

The study of small houses (by which I mean all houses below what may be briefly called the manor-house level, already adequately studied) is the classical example of a marriage between fieldwork and documents. The extraordinary wealth and variety of record material for this work are still not sufficiently realized, though in recent years there has been a gratifying flow of publications relating to probate inventories, the most important of the documentary sources.[1]

The Surtees Society published two volumes of North Country wills and inventories as long ago as 1835 and 1860, but the first volume to be solely devoted to household inventories (with a valuable introduction) was F. G. Emmison's *Jacobean Household Inventories* (Bedfordshire Historical Record Society, XX, 1938) which dealt with a Bedfordshire collection for the limited period 1617–20. In 1950 Francis Steer published *Farm and Cottage Inventories of Mid-Essex, 1635–1749* (Essex Record Office Publications no. 8). Like Emmison's book, it covered a limited field, in this instance two parishes only—Writtle and Roxwell. There is much to be said in any event for the close study of one or two parishes over a period of time.

In 1963 P. A. Kennedy published *Nottinghamshire Household Inventories* (Thoroton Society, Record Series, XXII). This collection again was necessarily limited by the sheer volume of the material available. It is confined to the Peculiar Court of Southwell (some 23 parishes) and it includes all the surviving inventories for the years 1512 to 1568, a remarkably full and early series.

In 1965 Elizabeth Melling and Anne Oakley published *Some Kentish Houses* (Kentish Sources V, Kent County Council) based largely upon probate inventories and glebe terriers for the sixteenth to eighteenth centuries, again with valuable notes.

Finally, in 1966, two volumes of inventories appeared, one for Oxfordshire covering the years 1550 to 1590, and the other of all the surviving Devon inventories, covering the period 1531 to 1699.[2]

[1] Nearly all the wills and inventories for the large diocese of Exeter were destroyed in an air raid in May 1942, the largest archive loss of the war in England. Those transcribed by Miss Cash survived unrecognized in another building. The majority fall into the period 1590–1699.

[2] I have discussed the value of probate inventories in this connexion more than once, notably in *Local History in England,* pp. 130–32, to which the reader is referred. A bibliography of printed collections of inventories is given in John West, *Village Records* (1962), pp. 129–31.

Despite this flow of volumes in recent years an enormous amount of value to the student of vernacular building remains unpublished and will indeed always remain so by reason of its vast extent. Thus the inventories for the diocese of Canterbury cover the period 1524–1857 (though mainly Elizabethan and Stuart), and amount to about 40,000 documents. In addition there are the inventories in the Consistory Court (1566–1759) and the Archdeaconry Court (1524–1857). The use made of a few of these records in *Some Kentish Houses,* already referred to, makes one wish for several volumes from these archives alone. Even the small county of Leicestershire has a collection of inventories from the early sixteenth century to the early nineteenth—but mainly 1550–1700—running into tens of thousands. Above all, we need published collections of inventories for the North of England, to facilitate the study of one of the most rewarding regions of all.

The value of these inventories to the fieldworker is manifold. To give only one example, they usually (though not always) list the rooms of a house by name and one gradually forms a general impression of the layout of houses of different periods and different social types which is an invaluable complement to the analysis of houses on the ground. We cannot always be sure from the inventories alone of the precise location of particular rooms in a large house or their exact relationship to each other. Nor, in studying a house on the ground, can we always be sure of the names and uses of the various rooms. But by bringing our inventory knowledge to bear upon the structures themselves we can usually identify all the rooms, their uses, and their relationship to each other.

While the vast majority of probate inventories are to be found in local record offices (or diocesan registries where they have not yet been transferred), one should not overlook the considerable collections that have found their way into the Public Record Office. These are located in:

Exchequer K. R. Files. E.154. Fully indexed
ditto   E.143. Not indexed
ditto   E.136. Not indexed
ditto   E.199. Not fully indexed

Chancery files.   C.131. Extents for Debts.
                                              Not fully listed.

In nearly all these classes of records the inventories are merely
a part of a larger collection. Similarly, one may find inventories
among the Special Commissions of Enquiry (Exch. K.R./E.
178. Fully indexed). Thus I found in this series an inquisition
into the possessions of one John Strobridge of Hooperhayne in
Colyton (east Devon) in 1576. This includes a full list of all his
household goods room by room, from which we discover that
his large farmhouse contained a hall, parlour, great chamber,
little chamber, closet, kitchen, buttery, chamber over the buttery, chamber over the kitchen, maids' chamber, and men's
chamber. We also get a list of the service-rooms and outbuild-
ings, informing us what to look for in an Elizabethan farmhouse on this scale. They included the 'new house with chamber
over', the 'brysshinge house' with a room over, malthouse,
'Wrynge house', brewhouse, out chamber, and the 'Cherse
house' [sic] whatever that may have been. The contents do not
help us here to decide: a pair of virginals, hangings, cushions,
mustard mill, garden rake etc.

Hooperhayne still stands as a farmhouse in Colyton parish
and much of this old house can be deciphered amid later
changes. But it must be said that even where probate inventories survive in considerable numbers for one parish or one
town, it is rarely that we can relate an inventory to a surviving
house. Sometimes it can be achieved, especially where an existing house carries the initials of the builder, inside or outside,
whose will and inventory can then (with a little luck) be traced.

GLEBE TERRIERS

With glebe terriers, which are descriptions of the house and
land (if any) belonging for the time being to the incumbent of a
parish, we are on surer ground. Like probate inventories, these
records vary in the amount of detail they give about the rooms
in the house. At their best they also go into detail about the
building materials. In many cases the buildings still survive,
and are of course readily identifiable from their nature. Such a

house survives, virtually unaltered, at Thorverton (Devon) where it is known today as The Old Parsonage. A terrier of 1613 describes it as containing a hall, a parlour, 'a little room within the Parlour' with a chamber over the same, a chamber over the parlour, a buttery with a chamber over it, a kitchen with a room over, 'a new house' [i.e. room] with a chamber over, and a 'little Dairy house.' Three cottages belonged to the glebe, together with a barn and a stall with a chamber at one end.

The terrier of 1680 describes the same house but goes into greater detail. In the Dwelling House there were three 'inner Rooms' a kitchen, a hall, and a parlour. The parlour floor was 'planched' (i.e. planked), the kitchen floor paved, and the hall floor, curiously enough, was of earth. There was 'one stone chimney' belonging to the parlour, and another in the hall. The kitchen chimney was built of cob (mud) as also was the rest of the walls. Adjoining the kitchen was a milk-house—this was the little dairy house mentioned in 1613—and there a little buttery 'within the parlour'. A cider-house stood at the northern end of the entry, and a little room adjoined the south side of the kitchen. There were five upper rooms, one of which was a study. There were fireplaces in the Parlour Chamber and the Hall Chamber (i.e. the bedrooms over those lower rooms). Altogether then the vicarage had five hearths, and could no doubt be identified in this way in the hearth tax assessments made in the third quarter of the seventeenth century.

The 1680 terrier is also useful in describing more fully the three cottages mentioned briefly in the earlier terrier. These were probably Elizabethan cottages in origin. One of them was fairly commodious with two lower rooms and two over, the whole built with mud (cob) and the roof thatched. Another had three lower rooms, but only one upper room, mud walls, one fireplace and a thatched roof. The third cottage had two lower rooms and one upper, a fireplace and mud walls. Here we have three cottages described, and all are different. It is clearly unwise to assume that cottages from the late sixteenth century onwards were of a standard size and type.

Thorverton vicarage was rebuilt on a new site in 1840. The

house described in these terriers, which had probably been built well back in the sixteenth century to judge by the surviving features, was divided into three cottages soon afterwards. But it is still known as the Old Parsonage and it stands on the street, retaining practically all its original features. Every room is identifiable from the terrier of 1613.

At Bratton Fleming in north Devon there were two glebe farms, Button (about 40 acres) and Castle (about 13 acres). The terrier of 1679 describes the parsonage house and the two farmhouses as follows: 'Parsonage house. The entrance being on the north. Over the gate is a little chamber plaistered and plancht with deel borrd. On the left hand is a stone wall (on which is a linnaye supported with three stone pillars) as far as the wall of the barn which, running north and south, is at the south end contiguous with the dwelling hous, which runs east and west and is entered into thorow a porch over which is a Study. On the left hand of the passage are three rooms the innermost the kitchen that next a pantry the third a tool hous floored with slatts over which are two rooms and the passage to the Study plancht with oaken borrd, the chambers divided with oaken studds and borrds, the passage from the lesser chamber with a daubing.

On the right hand of entry is a large Hall sealed at the higher end, paved axcepting the ascent which is laid with lime ashes. Next thereunto is a little parlour, parted from the Hall with studds and borrds, the floor of lime ashes over which is a chamber plaistered plancht with oaken borrd. Next a greater parlour plaistered and the floor made of lime ashes, over which is a chamber plaistered and plancht with oaken borrd. On the south side of which parlour is the brew house and privy. On the north side is the dayry with a chamber or the granary plancht with ashen borrd.

Next the Shipping and Stable parted beneath with a stone wall: from the Stable eastward to the gate is the mault house. Against the west wall of the Shipping are three hoggstys. All which houses are thatcht and walls built with stone.

Button houses. Two lower rooms divided with borrds. A Shipping adjoining to the first of the rooms on the north. A barn, a linnaye wherein is the stable, above which on the south is an old hous called the kitchin. Al the walls part of stone and part mudd and all the houses covered with reed.

Castle hous contains three lower roomes earthen floors divided with daubing on one little chamber, the roomes only washt with lime. At the west whereof is the stable annexed. On the south thereof the Shipping and on the east thereof is the barne. All which houses are covered with reed and the walls for the most of mudd.'

There is some reason to believe that the parsonage house was built in the third quarter of the sixteenth century. It was demolished in 1840 but sketches of it survive. Together with the detailed description of the 1679 terrier it should be possible to reconstruct the complete house of early Elizabethan days. The two farmhouses were probably of early date as neither of them had any upper rooms. The great value of these terriers for the study of houses on the ground is well evidenced in this Bratton Fleming document.

Very rarely one finds a plan going with the glebe terrier, as at Hardington (Somerset) in 1606. There is also one plan of an early parsonage (High Bickington) among the Devon glebe terriers at the county record office, and one in the Cornwall Record Office (St. Just).

Glebe terriers are equally valuable in the eighteenth and early nineteenth centuries, especially as many parsonage houses were rebuilt about then in new materials and on a new plan. Thus in the remote parish of Warleggan, on the southern edge of Bodmin Moor in Cornwall, the parsonage is described in 1613 as containing a parlour and a room over, a hall, a kitchen and a room over, a barn and a stable. This sounds very like a small medieval house, as the parlour and kitchen had chambers over; but the hall had none and was therefore open to the rafters. The terrier of 1727 says: 'The greatest part of the parsonage house being very ruinous was taken down and rebuilt by the present rector in 1707. It is now a hall and kitchen and chambers over them, a staircase and some small convenient rooms under it. The whole of stone and covered with slate. Hall 16 ft. by 13 ft., kitchen 11 ft. by 9 ft. By the staircase two closets, one of them the rector's study and the other for domestic use. Of the old buildings repaired by this rector are the parlour 14 ft. by 13 ft. now new flooring with deal, and the room over. In 1711 this rector built a new brewhouse. The barn contains four pairs of syles (crucks) which we apprehend to be bays of building.' So here much of the medieval house was rebuilt early in the eighteenth century, but some of it—the parlour end—was retained and renovated.

A glebe terrier made on 7th July 1638 describes the vicarage at Claybrook in Leicestershire at that date very briefly, and the lands and cottages belonging to it as glebe. The vicarage house, which was probably a sixteenth-century building, consisted of five bays; a barn of five bays stood beside it, together with a stable and 'two other little bayes of building', a garden, an orchard, and homestead, covering in all two acres of ground. A 'baye of building' was the distance between the principal upright timbers measured along the length of the house, and was usually sixteen feet. Claybrook vicarage was therefore a fairly commodious house, probably not eighty feet long but perhaps an L-shaped building with three bays along one side and a projecting arm of two bays. Most country cottages at this date were simple structures of two bays, that is about thirty-two feet in length, each bay forming one room—a 'house-place' or hall, and a bedroom (known then in Leicestershire as 'the parlour'). If there were a third bay, which was unusual in a cottage, it formed the kitchen.

Claybrook vicarage had two cottages belonging to it: 'one little cottage . . . in the occupation of Martin Knight, containing two bays of building, the rent for it yearly is three shillings and four pence a year'. And there was another cottage in the hamlet of Wibtoft 'in the occupation of Thomas Glover, containing three bays of building, the rent yearly is four shillings per annum.'

The glebe land consisted of three yardlands of arable meadow and pasture in the open fields, amounting to seventy-one acres, farmed by three of the parishioners for twenty pounds a year rent, and some other small pieces of meadow. These parcels of land are set out in great detail in the record, which contains dozens of the old field-names of three hundred years ago, before the enclosure of the parish.

Another survey of the vicarage house and glebe was made seventy years later, on 13th May 1708. This gives a very detailed description of the house, which had been rebuilt by parson Thorndike, in 1639, as 'the best parsonage-house in the country.'

'The Vicarage House', we are told, 'was erected by the learned Mr. Herbert Thorndike, containing eight bays. At the first entrance into it is a porch, and then a large space; on the right hand an hall and a pantry, both floored with boards; on the left hand a parlour and closet, both boarded. In the next bay is the stair-case on the left hand, and on the right a still-house, through which is the passage into a large cellar under the hall and pantry. The space leads into the kitchen, both of which are paved with bricks. On the right hand of the kitchen goes a space into the bakehouse; on the right hand of which is the dairy; on the left is the brewhouse, all floored with bricks. On the top of the stair-case, which is boarded, is a space, on the right hand of which is a chamber with a closet, both boarded; on the left hand another chamber with a closet, both plaster floors; and in the middle the vicar's study. From this stair-case goes another; at the top of it a garret, boarded floor; and forwards, two other garrets, one boarded, the other plaster; still up stairs a balcony covered with lead. From the stair-case aforenamed, on the right hand, is a chamber, boarded floor; forward is another chamber, with two closets, chamber plaster and one closet, the other boarded. From the stairs on the left hand of the kitchen is a chamber, boarded floor; on the right hand of which is another chamber, floored with plaster; and still on the right another chamber with a boarded floor. The house is timber building; one half is rough-cast, the other paved [i.e. filled in] with brick: the roof is covered tyles, all in good order.'

Outside the house, so well equipped with all the machinery for living a self-contained life—bakehouse, dairy, brewhouse, and kitchen—lay the barn (for the receipt of the tithes), the stables, and other outhouses.

'The Barn contains three large bays, mud walls, and covered with thatch; the stables three bays, mud walls, and covered with thatch; two bays of building for coals, &c. mud walls, and covered with thatch. The home-stall contains three acres, surrounded with lanes, and on the East with the green and church-yard; the garden walled round with mud walls; the court before the house with pales; the orchard next the green and church-yard with a mud-wall and hedge, and the other parts with quick; the back court with mud walls; the yard is walled next the church-yard and next the street with mud-walls; the other parts with buildings and quick; the kitchen garden on the North with the town street, on the West with a fish-ponds, on the South with a ditch and clipt hedge, on the East with the house and orchard.'

Then follows a description of the glebe lands, no longer scattered throughout the open fields but grouped in hedged fields which varied in size from three acres to twenty-three. Claybrook had been enclosed a generation earlier. The two cottages mentioned in 1638 had disappeared by this date.

In attempting to apply the description in a glebe terrier to an existing building, one must not forget that rooms may well have changed their uses in the course of generations. This is sometimes explicitly stated in terriers at different dates; and one can sometimes recognize in an old house on the ground a comfortable sitting-room which was once the kitchen. The existence of sideovens in such a room is good enough evidence. In the long house type, in which cattle formerly lived at one end, the cow-place (or shippon) has often been converted into a kitchen or a parlour and the cows are now housed in buildings erected in the yard.

One other caution should be uttered. The houses described in probate inventories and glebe terriers, whatever the date of the document, are not necessarily of that date themselves or anywhere near it. They may well have been a hundred or two hundred years old at the time the record was drawn up. Part of the local historian's task is to recognize these older types on the ground and in the archive room.

A necessary task is to make a complete building survey of a

parish or even a small town. If the probate inventories survive, and some parts of the country are much more rewarding in this respect than others, one should search out every one for a particular place or region and write a connected account of vernacular building over a period of time. I have attempted this in *The Midland Peasant,* in an excursus on Peasant Houses and Interiors, 1400–1800, relating to the Leicestershire village of Wigston Magna.[1] Coupled with such a documentary exercise, of course, one should make a thorough survey of houses surviving on the ground, not neglecting those of nineteenth-century date. Social habits and house-plans are changing so rapidly nowadays that nineteenth-century houses at all social levels should be planned and studied in detail while there is yet time.

HOUSES IN TOWNS

For small houses in towns there may well be additional records not commonly known to the student of vernacular building. I have discussed the modern records in chapter 4 (pp. 68–71). Where a borough owned property there should be a considerable collection of records (rentals, leases, and so forth) relating to houses and other buildings. Let me illustrate this from the city of Exeter which owned a large tract of land on the north of the city from time immemorial. In the closing decades of the sixteenth century building began to take place on this land, just outside the city walls. On one site described as a quarter acre of land in a survey made in 1564, a cottage was built some time in the 1570s. This is revealed by a rental of the following decade. In 1661 a fresh lease was granted to an Exeter merchant, from which it appears that the cottage had then disappeared, on condition that he built 'a decent and Convenient dwelling house' costing at least £60, and this house was duly erected. In 1815 the city fathers sold off the property to a Mr. Thomas Woodman, who took possession a year later

---

[1] The probate inventories relating to Wigston Magna run from 1529 to 1802, though they thin out quickly after 1730 and our knowledge thereafter must be gathered from surviving houses on the ground. Nevertheless the inventories describe no fewer than 160 houses in some detail. Similar studies ought to be made for villages, parishes, and towns in other parts of England.

and built a new house on the site which was completed in the year 1817. This house still stands, the third on the site. There is no trace of the former houses.

At Exeter also the Dean and Chapter owned a considerable amount of house property in the middle of the city, and their rentals and leases are invaluable for tracing the history of houses over a long period. Occasionally the older leases contain detailed descriptions of houses, and small plans showing their layout. Sometimes these plans can be matched up with existing buildings, as for example the plan of no. 7 The Close, which was the town house of the Courtenays, earls of Devon, for many generations. This was a fine example of a medieval town house. It still stands, somewhat adapted to the use of the Devon and Exeter Institution, but its original lay-out can be easily restored from the large-scale plan made in 1764.[1] Thus the archives of old boroughs and of cathedral bodies are particularly rewarding for the study of urban building. Indeed the larger houses in towns, those of former merchants, can hardly be understood without the use of the documentary evidence. These houses may well have differed somewhat in their basic plan from one region to another. Certainly they differed in their nomenclature for some of the rooms. The documents, in describing the houses of former centuries or generations, also enable us to work out any subsequent changes that may have been made. Often, for example, an old staircase has been replaced by a later one, with consequential changes in the rooms round about, and earlier inventories, leases, and plans will provide the clues as to what to look for.

The probate inventories also provide information about comparatively humble houses. In the Exeter city records we find descriptions of the houses of weavers, cordwainers, butchers, bakers, glaziers, and many other craftsmen and tradesmen of the Elizabethan and Stuart period. Most of these smaller houses have been pulled down long ago, but where the odd one survives the inventory is a valuable guide to its original size and plan.

[1] Since these lines were written, this plan has been published by Derek Portman in *Exeter Houses* 1400–1700 (University of Exeter, 1966).

So far we have been concerned in this chapter mainly with the documentary background to practical work on buildings. I have dealt with the practical side in *Local History in England,* pages 121 to 126, and the reader is referred to this for further guidance.

A great number of towns expanded rapidly in the course of the nineteenth century, not least some old cathedral cities. No fieldworker should neglect this period merely because it is thought to be recent and uninteresting. Photographs should be taken of every street down to say 1914, and plans made of the interiors of a representative sample of houses, both middle-class and working-class. With the great social changes of the last twenty years or so, what used to be called 'artisan housing' is becoming harder to find. It is important that it should be recorded for the benefit of posterity. Many houses built during the nineteenth century and the early twentieth were dated; all this should be recorded. Where no dated houses can be found in particular streets or roads, the borough records again will supply the precise answers. These sources have been discussed in chapter 4.

7

Farmsteads

The farmstead is perhaps the oldest form of human settlement. In England a great number of farms have been continuously occupied since at least Anglo-Saxon times, and a small proportion possibly since Iron Age times. Fieldwork and documentary research among farmsteads is much easier and more rewarding in those parts of the country where the farmstead or the hamlet has been the typical mode of settlement from the beginning. Thousands of existing structures are of considerable age, not a few surviving from the fifteenth century, and many from the late sixteenth and early seventeenth centuries. It is rare to find standing structures older than 1400, though the sites they occupy may have been inhabited for a thousand years or more.

Shortly after the Second World War ended, and I returned from civil servitude in the Great Wen, I was told of a farmhouse in mid-Devon which had apparently remained unchanged since it was built in the mid-sixteenth century. This was called Bartonbury, in the parish of Down St. Mary, and it stood alone far from the small village. It was indeed an almost unaltered specimen of a Tudor farmhouse. Documentary research enabled me to give it a fairly precise date, round about 1545, and I carried back its history as a farm to some time early in the eleventh century and by inference to a period well before that. If I set out the steps by which I compiled the history of this site, it will serve as a guide for a certain type of farm, though not for all. Nevertheless, many of the documents I shall cite are common to any farm in this kind of countryside of scattered settlement as distinct from 'village country'. Work upon Bartonbury was at first complicated by the fact that it did not get a separate name until the middle of the sixteenth century, but this difficulty was soon resolved.

As with private families with few or no records of their own, one begins historical research from the present and works backwards. There may come a point at which one can also go back to the beginning and work forwards, but at some juncture the two lines must meet as accurately as the boring of a long tunnel or it will be valueless as a piece of work.

Thus with a farm one should begin with the surviving deeds. The Bartonbury deeds did not go back a long way (though they were better than most) but they showed that in the eighteenth century the farm had belonged to the Dorset family of Sturt. In 1785 Humphrey Sturt esquire leased Bartonbury to John Stone. This was the earliest information to be gathered from the deeds of the property. The Stones farmed here for many years and bought the farm in 1799 out of the profits of wartime farming—a typical transaction in English farming history. In 1823 Mr. Henry Stone, yeoman, sold it to Benjamin Radford esquire of Chulmleigh for £2,800. It then amounted to 113 ac. 3 r. 19 p. The tithe map for Down St. Mary, dated 1845, shows Benjamin Radford as the owner. The occupier was Joseph Shobrooke, and the area was then 119 ac. 1 r. 23 p., so a field or two had been added in the intervening twenty years.

Directories for the latter part of the nineteenth century carry on the story. In 1857 Richard Cheriton was the occupier, but by 1878 there was no resident farmer and the old house was let as two cottages for a number of years. This comes from verbal information from the present farmer, Mr. Mortimer. The Radfords continued to own the farm down to 1918, when Mrs. Mary Radford sold it to Mr. T. H. Mortimer, to whose family it still belongs. In 1935 the farm had fallen in area to 86.414 acres, some 30-odd acres having been taken away previously by the Radfords and added to a neighbouring farm. In 1918 or thereabouts, the Mortimers took over the old farmhouse, which had—remarkably—escaped any important structural alteration during its use as two cottages.

Pursuing the history of the farm backwards from the earliest known date, 1785, the next step was to consult the land tax assessments among the Devon county records. But as these, like most such records in other counties, only survive from 1780, they did not add much to one's existing knowledge. The next step, however, took us back well over two hundred years. This was achieved by turning away from the particular records of the farm to the descent of the manor in which it lay—the manor of Down St. Mary.

The standard county history—Lyson's *Magna Britannia*—showed that Down St. Mary had formerly belonged to Buck-fast Abbey in south Devon. Monastic ownership usually means a long series of records. In this respect one is fortunate. The abbey was dissolved in 1539, and its possessions passed to the Crown, which valued its newly-acquired plunder in records known as Ministers' Accounts. These are now in the Public Record Office. The account for 1540 shows that in Down St. Mary and the neighbouring manor of Zeal Monachorum, which also belonged to the abbey, there were the usual free tenants and customary tenants, and also 'certain land called *le barton ground*' which was let to various local farmers. This was the former demesne land of the abbey, since in south-western England the word *barton* denotes a demesne farm.

The greater part of the monastic spoils had been sold off by the improvident Crown by the time Henry VIII died in 1547. The manor of Down St. Mary was sold on 11 June 1544 to Sir John Fulford of Fulford, a wealthy Devon squire, and Humphrey Colles, a Somerset lawyer who played a prominent part in the disposal of monastic lands. Included in this sale was 'the barton land leased to various tenants' at 32s 4d a year. This was the land now called Bartonbury. Whenever monastic land was sold off, it was properly valued and a market-price fixed at so many years' purchase. The details of these valuations, some fuller than others, are given in records known as Particulars for Grants. These are now in the Public Record Office (E.318), for the most part unpublished.[1]

Clearly, the abbey had never built a farmhouse here but had leased their demesne to neighbouring farmers who farmed it from their own buildings. Humphrey Colles acquired the manor from Sir John Fulford, and his descendants continued to own it until the second quarter of the seventeenth century, when an heiress carried it by marriage to the Sturts of Crichel in Dorset (Lysons). Pole, the Devon historian, writing about 1630 says that the manor of Down St. Mary then belonged to John Colles of Somerset, 'who hath conveyed it unto Margaret, his second daughter.' So it came into the Sturt family, who owned Bartonbury from then until 1799.

Bartonbury was identical with the abbey demesne land in Down St. Mary, and with one great jump we can go back as far as Domesday Book (1086) when the abbot of Buckfast had half a hide of land in his demesne with one plough. Before landing there, however, it is necessary to bring the farmhouse into the picture. It seems clear that when Humphrey Colles acquired the manor of Down St. Mary from Sir John Fulford in 1544, he decided to end the system by which the barton land was leased out to various tenants (which cannot have been the best sort of farming practice) and to build a house on the site and work the barton land as a distinct farm. So we get the new house of Bartonbury, *bury* being another word meaning the lord's land as distinct from village land. Every structural feature of the existing house suggests a date round about 1545–50.

We can now proceed backwards from Domesday Book, when Buckfast Abbey held the two manors of Zeal and Down together. The Hundred Rolls (1275) inform us under Zeal that the manor had been given to the abbey by Canute (1016–35) who had founded Buckfast in the year 1018. There can be little doubt that this statement is correct, and we may safely assume that the manor of Down St. Mary was given at the same time,

---

[1] Those for Devon have been edited by Dr. Joyce Youings and published by the Devon and Cornwall Record Society under the title of *Devon Monastic Lands: Calendar of Particulars for Grants 1536–58*. This class of record does not seem to be as well known as it should be among local historians and topographers.

the two manors forming at that date a single estate. So the land of Bartonbury was royal land long before the Norman Conquest and was given by Canute to Buckfast in or about the year 1018. It was owned by the abbey until 1539, and after a brief spell in royal hands again it was owned successively by the Colles, Sturts, and Radfords, until it came to the present owner in 1918. Indeed, one could take the history of the land back even farther, though imprecisely, by saying that this land had become royal property at the time of the Saxon conquest of Devon, which in this particular part of the county must have followed the successful battle at Posbury, not far away, in the year 661. But it may, of course, have been uncleared and unnamed territory at that date, with no identity of its own.

GENERAL SOURCES FOR FARM HISTORY

The sources used for compiling the above piece of farm-history do not exhaust the subject, and it is as well now to turn to a more generalized account which will include all the known sources for this kind of work.

The starting point should be the deeds of the property. In a number of cases the older deeds have found their way into the local County Record Office, especially where the farm has been part of some big estate and the owners have handed over all their papers. The deeds are of variable value in this respect. Sometimes they go no further back than about 1880. There may be two reasons for this disappointing run. One is that the Law of Property Act passed in 1925 reduced the period for proving title to property to thirty years. This meant that solicitors need no longer keep every scrap of parchment and paper relating to particular properties but only enough to prove title for a generation or so. The earlier deeds etc. were either handed over to the local Record Office, if the solicitor was an enlightened man, or simply destroyed in order to make more room in the office. The other reason for a disappointing run of deeds may be that the farm had been a part of some large estate and had been sold off in recent times. In this case it will not possess

an independent series of deeds,[1] but the estate papers should
contain, on the other hand, a series of leases of the farm to
various tenants for century after century. There should also be
periodic Rental Books and surveys, possibly even estate maps.

As an example of a fine run of deeds and leases, there is a
farm called Binneford, in the parish of Stockleigh English, in
the deep backwoods of Devon. This farm started at least a
thousand years ago as a separate freehold (it is named in a
Saxon charter) and eventually became part of a larger estate.
The records of this estate have been deposited in the city
record office in Exeter (they should really be in the county
record office) and begin as far back as *c.* 1180. From that time
onwards there are conveyances and leases for every century
down to the present day. Another farm called Halstow, in the
Devonshire parish of Dunsford, has a bundle of 39 deeds
relating to it, running from the thirteenth century to the end of
the eighteenth. A long run of documents like this will usually
contain a great deal of topographical information besides the
usual purely legal information about owner and tenants. Thus
the Halstow deeds contain information about the topography
of the farm—old field names, roads and streams, and so on—
as far back as the thirteenth century. They also contain the
names of local freeholders from all around who witnessed the
deeds. Deeds of 1539 and 1598, and others, give us details about
the sixteenth and seventeenth century farmhouse; and some of
the sixteenth and seventeenth century leases give us details
about the farming practice of the time.

In dealing with the possibilities of deeds and leases, we have
gone a little too far back into the past. On the assumption that
the surviving deeds are likely to be rather disappointing than
otherwise, the question arises: where do we go from the late or
mid-nineteenth century? Most of the records I shall cite now
will give some information, if only a crumb or two. The old
directories should be consulted. These take us back to the
period 1840–50 in most counties, occasionally a little earlier.

---

[1] Even where a farm had been absorbed into a large estate at some point in its
history, it may have enjoyed an independent existence before that and its early
deeds may therefore survive among the estate papers.

They should give information about owners and occupiers since that time, though at irregular intervals. Parish rate books, if they survive, will fill in the picture.

The next essential record is the tithe map and award, which generally date from the late 1830s or the early 40s, following the Tithe Commutation Act of 1836. There are or should be three copies of this map and award—one in the parish, one in the diocesan registry (now probably transferred to the local county record office), and one in the Tithe Redemption Commission in London. The most accessible copy is usually that in the local record office. For various reasons there may be no tithe map and award. This arises largely from differences in regional history. Thus the coverage of tithe maps and awards in Cornwall and Devon is nearly 100 per cent, and similarly in Kent and Shropshire. But in the East Midlands it may be as low as only a quarter or a third of the parishes. In Northamptonshire it is only 23½ per cent, in Leicestershire 31 per cent.[1] The main reason for this extreme difference is that those parishes which were enclosed by Parliamentary Act (chiefly in Georgian times) also took the opportunity of extinguishing their tithes at the same time, and so no tithe award was called for after 1836. In such parishes therefore we shall find conversely a high proportion of places possessing an enclosure award. Whereas Devon, Kent, and Cornwall have very high coverage in the tithe surveys, they have no coverage in the enclosure awards except for a limited amount of enclosure of commons and waste. On the other hand, Northamptonshire has an enclosure coverage of nearly 52 per cent, and Leicestershire some 38 per cent. Theoretically, therefore, what one has lost in the mid-nineteenth century is compensated by the existence of an earlier record. In practice, however, the enclosure map is often missing. There should be one with every award, but for some reason a considerable number of these maps have been lost whereas the award has been treasured as an important legal document.

The tithe map and award give one the name of the owner

For a detailed discussion of the tithe surveys and their value as a source for farming history, see H. C. Prince, 'The Tithe Surveys of the Mid-Nineteenth Century' in the *Agricultural History Review*, vol. VII, Part 1 (1959).

and occupier of every farm, the acreage of every field, its name, and to use to which it was then put. The map, usually on a very large scale, contains a great deal of other topographical information about the village and its buildings, and the other features of the parish. It could well be made the basis for a topographical exploration of the parish as it was a hundred and thirty years ago and as it is today.

Whether or not we possess the enclosure map and award, the next step is to examine the Land Tax Assessments. Most counties have a complete run of these records from 1780 to 1832. Some counties, for example Suffolk, apparently have none until late in the nineteenth century. Others possess a few inconsecutive assessments back to the early years of the eighteenth century, besides their main series. These assessments normally tell one the name of the owner of a farm, and the occupier if any. In 'village country' where farms are not often identified by name, it still requires some acumen to sort out a particular farm; but in parishes consisting mainly of scattered farms these are usually distinguished by name. The same remarks apply to parish rate-books, which may survive back to the late sixteenth century and furnish a splendid directory of all the people of the parish except the very poor.[1]

It should be possible then to trace the history of any farm back to 1780, and to a somewhat earlier period if there is a parliamentary enclosure award of an earlier date. The difficulties begin beyond that date, if there are no deeds or leases or estate rentals to help one. Occasionally the parish register of baptisms, marriages, and burials gives the names of the farms of various people when an entry is made, especially where there are two people of the same name, but this is uncommon.

Among other records to be searched are the Hearth Tax Assessments, most of which are in the Public Record Office and are unprinted. Occasionally again the local county record office possesses a few hearth tax returns. They run from 1662 to 1674, i.e. the assessments which give names of occupiers. The

[1] For example, there is a full assessment for the parish of East Down in north Devon made in the year 1589, giving the name of every farm at that date and of its occupier. It also gives the quantity of oats payable by each farmer and cottager to the churchwardens, presumably as some special levy.

tax itself was not repealed until 1689 but the later assessments do not give names. Nor do any of the assessments give the names of farms, only of villages or parishes. Thus one must know the name of the occupier at this period in order to trace his house from these records. If one knows this, the record will tell one indirectly something about the size of the house. If for example the farmhouse was rated at four hearths in 1664, it should be possible to trace these fireplaces. Some may now be blocked up, or it may be that the house has been enlarged or reduced in size since the 1660s; but at least there is something to go upon beyond surmise.

A useful collection of records not generally known to students of houses and property-history are the Deeds of Bargain and Sale, sometimes simply referred to as Enrolled Deeds. These were enrolled with the Clerks of the Peace in the counties as a result of a statute of 1536. They tend to be copious for the remainder of the sixteenth century and to fade out after the early seventeenth. In Devon there are more than two thousand such deeds and many farms are nicely documented. The enrolled deeds for Somerset have been published. Most counties, however, seem to have a very imperfect collection, Essex having only one roll of 100 deeds covering the period 1536–1624, while those for Kent do not begin until 1596.

Manorial records may be of considerable help if the farm in question was held otherwise than by freehold. In manor court rolls and manorial surveys and rentals, freehold farms were naturally of little interest to the lord of the manor or his steward and so receive the scantiest mention. But a farm held by copyhold or leasehold may be traceable over a long period if the necessary records survive.

Farms which were handed over at some date as part of the endowment of a charity, such as a hospital or a school, may produce a particularly long and useful series of records. Here the searcher is fortunate beyond the average. Thus when William Wyggeston founded the Hospital which bears his name, in 1521, he endowed it inter alia with four farms in the village of Wigston Magna and handed over all the deeds and and other legal documents relating to them. These go back to the late twelfth century, and it is therefore possible to trace the history of each of these farms from that time until the present day.[1]

Finally, in some parts of England, and notably in the south-west, a great number of farms are named individually in Domesday Book, and a few of these are named even earlier in Saxon land charters. In some cases it is possible to say something about the history of a site back to the late seventh century. These ancient farms should be examined on the ground, paying attention to such important factors as the water-supply, the aspect of the site, the soils, the lay-out of the farm in relation to the homestead, and so forth.

Though nothing will remain above ground of the older structures on the site (it is rare to find anything older than the fifteenth century) the whole complex of the site should be examined, i.e. the position of the dwelling-house in relation to the other farm-buildings, the relationship of the farm-buildings to each other, and the use of the buildings. In cattle-raising country, the farmstead will usually be the focus of a number of tracks leading into the yards. All these should be noted on the map, and checked on the tithe-map also, which may show tracks that have since gone out of use.

I am conscious of the fact that most of my examples have been drawn from the Midlands and south-west England. The problems of farm-continuity and of topography generally may be different in south-eastern England, above all perhaps in Kent, and perhaps in East Anglia where the unusual pattern of settlement and of manorial geography requires an expert local knowledge. The basic records for this kind of exploration and research are the same, but the topographical problems may well be very different.

---

[1] See my book *The Midland Peasant* (1957) for fuller details about these farms. Their lands were of course reshuffled at the enclosure in 1767, but the farmhouses remained on the same site in Bullhead Street.

8

Hedges and Walls

I recall again Maitland's words, written some seventy years ago, which I have already quoted: 'Much remains to be done before we shall be able to construe the testimony of our fields and walls and hedges. . . .' One can date certain kinds of hedge-banks from records of one sort and another, and having dated them can proceed to identify others for which no documents exist. I have, for example, dated certain massive hedge-banks in mid-Devon from a Saxon boundary charter as belonging to the late seventh century; others from manorial documents as being boundaries of probably the tenth or eleventh century; and so on right down to the hedges of the parliamentary enclosure movement in the time of George III, or a little earlier and a little later. It is possible to calculate for some parishes, with sufficient records, the mileage of hedges at different dates, and even to recognize different ages of hedge-banks, though not to date them very closely as yet. There is at least one hedge-bank in mid-Devon which I think is probably Romano-British in date, since it is referred to in a Saxon boundary-charter of the tenth century as 'the old dike' and it lies near a farm with a Celtic name.

For some years now, knowing the extremely variable dates of hedge-banks in the English countryside, I thought that hedges of different dates—ranging all the way from the second century to the nineteenth,—should theoretically show significant differences in their vegetation, and that it should be possible to arrive at an approximate date for hedges from a close examination of their constituent vegetation where one had no documentary date for them.

I remember noticing many years ago in a small piece of mid-Devon which I used to study intensively how the boundary of a hundred ran for some distance along the edge of a wood, and then followed a continuous hedge-bank. Since the hundred as an institution dates from the early tenth century, this boundary was at least a thousand years old. It occurred to me then, knowing no botany whatsoever, that hedge-banks of such antiquity ought to show considerable differences in their vegetation from more modern hedges; that along the edge of a wood, for example, one might find vegetation that was really a hang-over, as it were, from ancient woodland. But I could not pursue this idea for lack of any botanical knowledge.

MAPPING HEDGE-BANKS

However, in recent years, Dr. Max Hooper of the Nature Conservancy hit upon the same idea and was able to pursue it actively, with exciting results. I am indebted to Dr. Hooper for permission to quote some of his preliminary results in various counties, but it must be understood that these results may be subject to modification as the work goes on. Basically the method of estimating the age of a hedge-bank is simple: one counts the number of shrub species in a sample 50 to 100 yard length. Certain hedge-banks can be firmly dated from documents, and this is the starting-point for establishing a hedge-chronology. Results obtained so far suggest that hedges of 100 years' age will have one shrub-species; those of Tudor times will have four species; those of Saxon times nine to twelve species. In other words, a hedge will contain one shrub species for every hundred years of life. This theory sounds too simple to be true, and doubtless it will require modification for different soils and perhaps different climates. Some possible modifications of the formula are considered later in this chapter.

The simplest method of attack in the field is to draw maps of the hedge-lines in the chosen parish or district at the different dates for which records are available. Maps of Buckworth (Huntingdonshire) for the period about 1700 to 1963 are given as an example (Map III). We are accustomed to think of our hedgerows as being a fairly permanent feature of the landscape, until very recent times at least; but those of Buckworth show remarkable changes at different dates. It may well be an exceptional parish in this respect. I would not expect the parishes of south-western England, for example, to show anything like this rapidity of change; though even here change is taking place today. Thus it was calculated in 1851 that there were in Devon some 28.6 miles of hedges to every square mile of land. In 1962 this mileage had fallen to less than 20. In Huntingdonshire the destruction of hedges is even more rapid. In 1850 there were rather more than 10 miles of hedge to every square mile. Now (1965) there are only three. The maps of Buckworth show how great the changes have been even since 1945.

In drawing such a series of hedge-maps the Ordnance Survey is the obvious point of departure. The field-pattern of today can be got from the most recent edition of the 6-inch map, supplemented where necessary by personal observation. The next step is to consult the first edition of the 6-inch or 25-inch maps and to draw the pattern of eighty to a hundred years ago. The maps of county Durham were published for example, in 1854–7, those of Norfolk between 1879 and 1886. The 25-inch survey was made between 1853 and 1893, the 6-inch maps being derived from it. Each map bears the date of its actual survey.

It is not generally known that the field-books (manuscript surveyors' drawings) survive from the first survey for the 1-inch map, which was made from 1795 to 1873. Actually most of the country south of a line from Preston to Hull had been surveyed by 1840. Many of the surveyors' drawings, now deposited in the Map Room of the British Museum, show field-boundaries on a larger scale (2 in., 3 in., or 6 in.) than the subsequent printed map; but in some cases these are diagrammatic and should be interpreted cautiously.[1]

Tithe maps are another valuable source for hedgerow maps in the nineteenth century. These maps were made following the Tithe Commutation Act of 1836, and therefore mostly date

---

[1] See a useful articule by J. T. Coppock, 'Changes in Farm and Field Boundaries in the Nineteenth Century' in *The Amateur Historian*, vol. III part 7 (1958).

MAP III **Buckworth** (Hunts) hedge patterns from 1700 to 1963

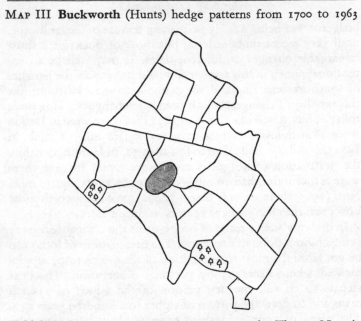

Field boundaries: *circa* 1700 (*redrawn from ms by Thomas Norton*)

Field boundaries: *circa* 1835 (*redrawn from Tithe Apportionment Map*)

Hedges: 1945 (*drawn from aerial photograph*)

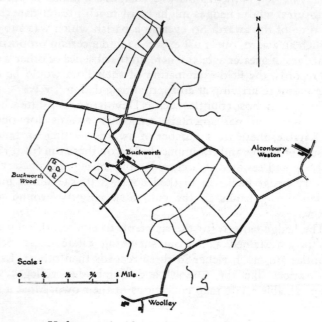

Hedges: 1963 (*drawn from aerial photograph*)

from the late 1830s and the early 1840s. The coverage of these maps, as we have seen, varies greatly from county to county.

Enclosure maps, even where they can be traced, cause some difficulties for the mapping of hedgerows. In the first place, they will show only the boundaries of each man's allotment in the Enclosure Award, not the boundaries of each field as he subsequently made them. If the award, for example, is dated 1786, it usually stipulated that the boundary fences of each allotment should be made within twelve months of the award, but it left each man free to subdivide this allotment internally as and when he liked. Thus the internal hedgerows of a particular allotment of 1786 may be considerably later than this date. This is not an important point in practice, as the dating of hedgerows from an examination of their flora cannot be precise within a matter of fifty years, and even longer the farther back one goes.

Another complication, of more practical importance, is that at the time of many parliamentary enclosure awards there already existed in the majority of villages a number of 'ancient enclosures' whose hedges might be of much greater date than the time of the award. So even in a parish which was subject to such an award, one must expect to find a certain proportion of hedges of greater age; and here, in the absence of other written records, the field-examination of their flora would be the only means of arriving at an approximate dating.

Further, in those counties such as Devon or Shropshire where there were no parliamentary enclosure awards for open-field arable, there are a number of awards relating to the enclosure of wastes and commons. In Devon these run from 1802 to 1874, and resulted in a considerable mileage of nineteenth-century hedge-banks in marked contrast to the much more ancient hedge-banks in the cultivated country around and below.

The hedge-pattern for the sixteenth to eighteenth centuries can be ascertained also from surviving estate maps. Some counties are much richer in these records than others, Large landowners like the Oxford and Cambridge colleges will have valuable estate map collections of their own. Most if not all of these show field boundaries, though in open-field country this is not very helpful as the bulk of the map will be occupied by unhedged strips. Nevertheless, for a substantial part of England there exist large-scale estate maps from the late sixteenth century onwards which show field-boundaries in the form of hedgerows, and these can be plotted on to the modern large-scale map so as to show the intervening changes.

Such large-scale estate maps are rare before the last twenty years of the sixteenth century. Before that date it is doubtful if we can ever get a complete picture of the hedge-pattern for any parish from written records alone, though in some cases early surveys and leases (especially among monastic records) may be informative, provided one can locate the land referred to with certainty. Thus a lease among the Tavistock Abbey muniments relating to a field called Furze Close on a farm called Woodovis (in the parish of Tavistock) specifies in the year 1465 that a ditch shall be dug around the ground four feet wide and four feet deep, and the earth thrown up into a bank all round so making a new enclosure. This hedge-bank was then planted with quickset and coppice wood, and Nature has added to the flora during the last five hundred years. The Tavistock Abbey records also show that some of these early enclosures were up to 25 to 40 acres in area, and that there was a later tendency to subdivide them. Two fields on a farm called Bow-rish consisted of 12 and 20 acres respectively in 1491, but the lease is endorsed with a note that each had since been divided into three fields. They remain as six fields to this day.[1] From what has been said it is clear that the hedgebanks will be of different dates, how different we do not know without an examination in the field.

Other hedge-banks dating from medieval times can be traced, with some difficulty at times, from records known as forest perambulations and from licences for the making of parks for hunting. Occasionally these records are specific enough to enable one to trace the boundaries directly on to a map; but sometimes one has to find them laboriously in the field (see chapter 3). Whichever way one does it, one then obtains a

[1] Finberg, *Tavistock Abbey* (1951), pp. 50-1.

dated hedge-bank, and its flora can be examined in order to see what sort of pattern it makes.

For mapping the hedge-lines of an older period than the medieval, one must resort to an interpretation of the Ordnance maps. Thus parish boundaries—taking care that they are the ancient ecclesiastical boundaries and not those of modern civil parishes—may be regarded as mostly pre-Conquest in date. Where they are demarcated therefore by hedge-banks we may date those hedge-banks as of pre-Conquest origin, or at least immediately post-Conquest. Probably most ecclesiastical parishes had been demarcated by the twelfth century. Some parish boundaries, those of mother-parishes for instance, may date from well back in the Anglo-Saxon period.

A few hedge-banks of Anglo-Saxon date, or even perhaps earlier in rare cases, may be traced from pre-Conquest land charters. Thus a charter relating to a grant of land by King Edward the Martyr to Aelfsige at Cheriton Bishop in Devon, issued in the year 976, refers at one point to 'the old *dic.*' This *dic*, which can be identified today, is a hollow way running between two earthen banks which must be contemporary in date with the ditch or hollow way. The question is 'how old was 'old' in 976?' As the land in question has a Celtic name (Treable) and a coin of the second century has turned up in one hedge-bank on this farm, we may assume that the earthen bank on the western side at least was Romano-British in date. Apart from this exceptional example, Anglo-Saxon land charters, carefully worked out, will produce a number of authentic hedge-banks constructed during that period.

HEDGE-BANKS AND THEIR FLORA

Once the hedge-bank map has been drawn from all or some of the above sources, it becomes possible to apply the botanical method more fruitfully than merely by plunging into the countryside without any such documentary preparation. Indeed in most kinds of fieldwork it is advisable to study all available documents in the first place, or much time is wasted and false theories are formed which it is sometimes difficult to eradicate afterwards. In my own experience the most fruitful sequence has been: documents—fieldwork—back to the documents—field-work again. Only in rare cases are there no documents at all to be studied; or it may be that a discovery is first made in the field which leads one back to a search for any relevant documents.

What we enter the field with is likely to be a hedge-map with a good deal of information upon it and also a great number of gaps, i.e. hedge-banks and hedgerows for which no documentary dating is possible. Armed with a suitable list, of trees and shrubs (see below) one examines a sample 50 to 100 yards length of hedge on *both* sides, ticking off on the list all those species which are found. The tentative formula of one species for every hundred years of life should be tested against any firm documentary dating and a local chronology established. From this one can proceed to date all the hedge-banks for which no documents are available, and these will be—in most parishes —the majority of the hedges.

The common names of trees and shrubs that may be found in English hedges and lanes are:

Alder Buckthorn	Elm
American Bellbine	Field Bindweed
Ash	Gorse
Barberry	Great Bindweed
Beech	Guelder Rose
Bird Cherry	Hawthorn
Bittersweet or Woody	Hazel
Nightshade	Holly
Black Bryony	Honeysuckle
Black Nightshade	Hornbeam
Blackthorn	Horse Chestnut
Bramble	Ivy
Bush Vetch	Maple
Cherry Plum	Oak
Crab Apple	Poplar
Dogwood	Privet
Downy Birch	Purging Buckthorn
Elder	Rowan

Sessile Oak	Wayfaring Tree or Hoarwithy
Silver Birch	White Bryony
Spanish Chestnut	Wild Cherry
Spindlewood	Wild Roses
Sycamore	Willow
Travellers Joy	Woodland Hawthorn
Tufted Vetch	Woodruff

It will help at this point if some specific examples are given from Devon.

In the parish of Bratton Fleming in north Devon the moors to the east of the village rise to rather more than 1,000 feet above sea-level at Bratton Down; and at Mockham Down, in the adjacent parish of Charles to a similar height. On these uplands the hedges are straight, forming regular-shaped fields, and consist of almost pure beech, with an occasional willow or elder. On the hundred-year theory, these hedges would be 100 ± 50 years old. In point of fact, Bratton Down was enclosed in 1841 (enclosure award in the Devon county records) so that the hedges here would be about 125 years old. No award can be traced for Mockham Down, but the enclosure here was about the same date.

To the west of Bratton Fleming village, on much lower ground, there is a very different history. A long ridge of land, nearly a mile wide and about two miles long, and between 500 and 600 feet above sea-level, contained originally two ancient farms called Chelfham and Chumhill (see Map IV). The boundary between Chumhill and the rest of Bratton Fleming is marked by a considerable ditch (A to B on the sketch map) which appears as a lane on the 2½-inch map. From B to C is a steep and narrow lane. Apart from a kink at B, where it crosses an old road, this line A—C is marked by a continuous hedge-bank. Such a continuous line, not crossed by other hedges but used by them as a *terminus ad quem*, is itself evidence of great antiquity, especially running as it does direct over the ridge from one stream-boundary to another. The western boundary of Chumhill (D—E on the sketch map) is also a continuous hedge-bank, four-fifths of a mile long

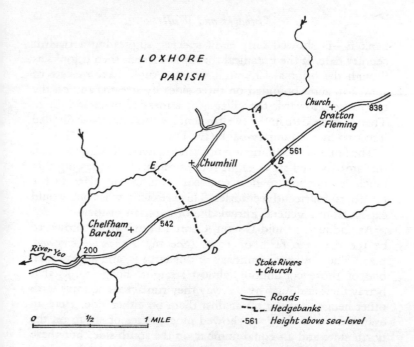

MAP IV Ancient hedgebanks at Bratton Fleming (Devon)

Both Chelfham and Chumhill are first mentioned in documents in the 1230's and not before. Nevertheless, Domesday Book tells us that 'three small manors'—not named—had been incorporated into Bratton between 1066 and 1086, and there is some reason to suppose that two of these were Chelfham and Chumhill. One other documentary clue is offered by the place-name Chumhill: it means 'Cēomma's spring,' Cēomma being an Old English personal name.

A botanical examination of the two boundary-banks (A—C and E—D) produced some valuable evidence as to the age of the estate, but also raised (as so often happens) a further question that remains to be solved. The eastern hedge-bank of Chumhill produced eleven shrub-species, indicating a boundary going back to the tenth century (say 850–950 A.D.) and so confirming the pre-Conquest origin of the manor. But the hedge-bank E—D showed only eight species, suggesting a twelfth century date. If the botanical theory is correct, then it looks as though the original Chumhill was an Anglo-Saxon estate of some 830 acres bounded on three sides by streams and on the fourth side, towards the village, by a massive bank and ditch. Then at some date in the twelfth century this estate was divided into two by a boundary-bank (E—D).

The botanical examination of certain internal hedge-banks in this area showed six to eight species of shrub, suggesting that much reclamation or new enclosure was taking place in the twelfth to fourteenth centuries. This is exactly what one would expect from a general knowledge of agrarian history.

At Cadbury, in mid-Devon, Church Farm can be shown to be the demesne farm of 1066. (See my *Provincial England*, p.22.) The southern boundary of this farm is, and always was, one of those continuous, almost straight, hedge-banks that betray their antiquity by the way they run across country with other hedges butting up against them on either side. Here an examination of the flora showed nine species of shrub on the north side, and an equal number on the south side; but there were slight differences between the species. Altogether there were eleven different species in this hedge-bank, suggesting a date of about 900 A.D. for its construction. Other hedges in the same area had nine species (equivalent to a date of about 1100), but a few had only four. So here we seem to have an early hedge-pattern with Tudor additions, perhaps making large fields smaller for better farming as we saw in the Tavistock example already cited.

On the other hand a hedge-bank recorded in a charter of 976 had only eight species, and a hedge-bank at the eastern end of the Raddon Hills, marking the boundary of an estate given to Exeter Abbey in the early tenth century, also had eight.

Here is a wonderful new field of inquiry for the local historian. Not only must he examine the houses and other buildings of his chosen territory but, in the countryside at least, he must examine all the hedges also if he is to write a true local history.

There are, however, important questions to be settled before the formula (or more strictly, hypothesis) of one shrub to every hundred years can be applied to a given terrain. It may be that there is an upper limit to the number of species in any hedge, however old: that beyond a certain age, still to be determined, a hedge-bank does not go on adding to its variety. So a Devonshire hedge-bank with, say, eleven different species may be much older than 1,100 years.

Moreover, there are thirty possible shrub species in eastern England, but only twenty-five to the west of the river Parrett, the eastern frontier of south-west England. So a hedge-bank in Devon or west Somerset with ten species out of a possible twenty-five may be older than a Huntingdonshire hedge with ten out of a possible thirty species. This raises the whole question of the influence of soil and climate on flora. At Radworthy (Devon), some 1,200 feet above sea-level on Exmoor, there are many small enclosures of great but unknown age. As Radworthy is recorded in Domesday Book as *Radeuda* (= Raeda's farm) some of the hedge-banks here must be Saxon in date. Except for two recently occupied plots whose hedges have a few beech and hawthorn plants, the hedge-banks show no shrubs except Ling (*Calluna vulgaris*) and a Heath (probably *Erica cinerea* or possibly *E. Tetralix*). The same applies to what is probably a deserted hamlet site overlooking the Bray valley near Kipscombe in Bratton Fleming parish.[1] Here, too, many of the hedge-banks must be at least medieval in date. It is clear that soil and climate—here very wet and bleak for a good part of the year—play a large part in determining the flora of these sites; though one also wonders, as an historian, whether the fact that they have been deserted for so long may not have encouraged ling and heather to overcome whatever flora there may have been under a different farming regime.

Local historians, armed with a hedge-map for different periods, and accompanied by an expert botanist friend, can do much to further this new line of research by correlating age and flora, soil and flora, management and flora, and so on. As to management, for example, it is possible that Tudor enclosers actually planted mixed hedges rather than the single species (the hawthorn) favoured by the enclosers of the eighteenth century.

[1] Information supplied by Mr. Charles Whybrow, of Bratton Fleming, Devon.

Barnaby Googe's *Foure Bookes of Husbandry*, published in 1601, implies that Tudor enclosers planted mixed hedges, so starting off, as it were, with a number of ready-made species. And in the old wooded areas of England, to introduce another complication, many hedge-banks, particularly where they form parish or hundred boundaries, may well be remnants of mixed woodland which had half a dozen species in them from the start. Thus the local historian-cum-botanist must carefully construct his own chronology while keeping the 100-year-per-shrub hypothesis as a working rule at least to begin with.

FIELD WALLS

In those parts of the country where stone walls form the boundaries of fields rather than living hedges, there are fewer possibilities for dating with any degree of precision. Clearly the examination of flora offers little to go on, though I do not entirely rule out the possibility that medieval stone walls, like the granite walls of Dartmoor, might yield in sheltered spots some evidence in their flora to the trained eye. But in general we have to proceed by studying their basic pattern, the field-shapes they enclose, and their methods of construction. The best introduction to this subject is Dr. Arthur Raistrick's *Pennine Walls*. One sees the possibilities of the subject merely by juxtaposing maps showing different field-wall patterns. At Hebden and other places in the West Riding the closes 'make . . . irregular, crazy patterns near the villages—each tenant walling in a portion, usually from half to one acre, occasionally a little more, making his wall where it was convenient, winding a little to include large boulders and blocks of stone, or going at a curve to meet some other wall or fence. In these older walls, it is common to find their base including monstrous single blocks and boulders, often a ton or more in weight, two or three feet high and as much long, standing on edge like rows of giant teeth. The wall includes and is built on to them. Partly from first design and largely by age such walls are curly and bulging, hardly a straight line to be found among them.'

In the sixteenth and seventeenth centuries, when a good deal

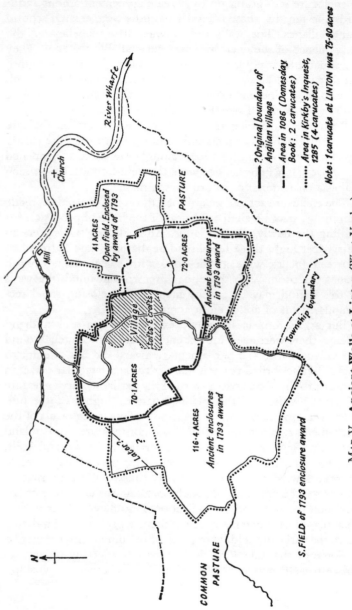

MAP V Ancient Walls at Linton (West Yorks.)
(based on a reconstruction by Dr. Arthur Raistrick.)

of enclosure was going on by private agreement among land-lords and tenants, these irregular patterns were created around many villages. The walls follow very little plan beyond the convenience of the enclosure and the available material. They are squat and irregular, of great thickness in stony ground, aimed partly at clearing the soil of stones, and added to from time to time. There is little coursing of the stones in the wall, nor any regularity of size (Raistrick, *op. cit.* p. 9).

With the parliamentary enclosure movement of the late eighteenth and early nineteenth century there was 'the steady development to straight ruled walling'—precisely as happened in landscapes where hedges were the field-boundaries—which makes a characteristic pattern on the map.

The enclosure act and award for Linton in Wharfedale, made in 1792–3, may be cited as typical of the kind of provision for walling the newly allotted lands. All enclosing walls were to be six feet high, three feet broad at the base, and battered to fourteen inches wide at the top, with twenty-one through stones per rood. With these measurements in mind, the walls of this period may be readily identified, enclosing small rectangular fields of about eight acres in size.

But at Linton, as in nearly every northern and midland village, there were also 'ancient enclosures' immediately around the village which the parliamentary award did not attempt to touch. These form a pattern like a 'drunken irregular maze' in contrast to the geometric pattern of the parliamentary enclosure of the 1790s. Beyond this planned pattern, higher up the hill-sides, yet another pattern is detectable. This is the result of the parliamentary enclosure of the common pastures and upland grazings. Here, too, the walls are straightly drawn and built, but they cut the moor up into long strips up to thirty acres or more in size, and some of them may run straight for a mile or more over the uplands. Generally speaking the enclosure of the common pastures and upland moors is somewhat later in date than that of the open fields below them, a great deal of it dating from the early and middle decades of the nineteenth century.

Some of the upland walls may be considerably older than this, especially where they form boundaries between townships.

As population grew in the twelfth and thirteenth centuries, and more and more of the upland grazings came into use, disputes broke out between adjoining townships as to their respective rights along an undetermined frontier. Dr. Raistrick cites two such examples from the Yorkshire moors, one a dispute between the tenants of Fountains Abbey and those of Sawley Abbey, and the other a dispute between Fountains and Bolton Abbeys. Monastic cartularies and deeds will often reveal evidence of such disputes which resulted in some visible change in the landscape, such as the building of a frontier wall, and so present a nice problem in fieldwork for the student of today.

Many of the small enclosures surrounding old villages must be, not merely sixteenth century in date, but considerably older. At Linton again, not far from Grassington in Wharfedale, Dr. Raistrick has observed a piece of ancient history from the way some old walls run, and the way in which they are constructed. In Domesday Book, Linton was assessed at two carucates. Later records show that the carucate was 75 to 80 acres, so that we have to look for an eleventh-century area of about 150–160 acres within some boundary walls. These can be detected within the area described as 'ancient enclosures' in the enclosure award of the late eighteenth century, adding up to about 142 acres plus the area covered by the tofts and crofts of the village.

Not only this, but within this eleventh-century enclosure yet another wall runs continuously around the village, enclosing about 70 acres plus the village itself. This wall is of the most primitive and massive construction, with no through stones. It rests upon massive blocks of stone and is 4 to 5 feet thick at the base. It rises to $5\frac{1}{2}$ to 6 feet in height, and contains individual stones as much as 4 ft. × 3 ft. × 2 ft. thick, obviously the result of land clearance.

Other enclosure-walls run up to it and butt on to it, but nowhere break through it. It is clearly a boundary wall that was erected before anything else, and there can be little doubt it represents the first boundary wall of the Anglian village of the eighth century or thereabouts, protecting not only the tofts and crofts but also some 70 acres of farmland which was cleared of surface stones for the building of the wall. Two purposes were thus served at the same time. Some of this wall may be of the original construction, though it has necessarily been repaired from time to time. Most of what now stands is at least medieval in date, and basically it is the aboriginal wall of Linton.

In the record known as Kirby's Inquest (1285) Linton is given an assessment of four carucates—a doubling of the area since 1086—and once again we can find enclosures totalling about 157 acres within the area designated on the map which may represent the fields brought into cultivation in the two hundred years between Domesday and the later Inquest. These walls are all shown in a tentative map (Map V).

Even less has been written about stone walls than about hedgerows, but some of the methods of fieldwork are the same in each case. All walls for which there is a known or approximate date should be examined carefully for details of their construction, noting in a sketch-book different kinds of walling, the shape and size of the stones, and how they are placed one on another. As Dr. Raistrick says, one will then learn to recognize walling of different periods and even the work of individual craftsmen.

WHY DATE WALLS AND HEDGES?

It might be asked: has the dating of hedges and walls anything more than an antiquarian interest? Even if it had only an antiquarian interest it would still be a valuable and worthy exercise, for it would tell us a good deal about the way in which the landscape as we see it slowly came into existence, and we should recognize the work of our forefathers and enjoy it for its own sake. But from a wider point of view, that of the economic historian, the more or less exact dating of boundary hedges and walls will tell us a good deal about the agrarian history of the past which the records nowhere reveal. Using documents in the first place in order to get 'dated' examples, one proceeds from the known to the unknown, and discovers eventually how the field-pattern of a parish or a district was built up step by step. Not only that but we shall learn much about the changes in farming and about the settlement-history of the area. The history of field-patterns in England and Wales is much more diversified and complicated than was thought when H. L. Gray wrote his seminal book *English Field Systems* in 1915. Local historians who wish to familiarize themselves with the main trends of recent research in this territory should read H. P. R. Finberg's admirable paper in *Geografiska Annaler*, vol. XLIII (1961), entitled 'Recent Progress in English Agrarian History.' The argument about the origins, extent, and varied forms of the old open-field system continues in various places, in local antiquarian journals, in the *Economic History Review*, and in *Past and Present*, to name the most important sources.

We now know that English field-systems were infinitely more varied in character than had ever been supposed, that some of them were very localized in type, and that some are very deceptive in appearance when portrayed on late maps (such as the tithe maps), having changed from something totally different within a few generations. Customs of inheritance have played a considerable part in determining local field-patterns. In the patient building-up of knowledge about English and Welsh field systems, the local fieldworker has an important contribution to make.

9

Roads and Lanes

EARLY TRACKWAYS

Much has been written about the roads of England, many books and innumerable articles in the proceedings and transactions of local historical societies. But any fieldworker who has studied the roads, lanes, and paths of his parish or of a wider area knows that a great deal remains to be discovered before we have anything like a complete story. Even in well-trodden subjects like Roman roads there is endless work to be done, as Mr. I. D. Margary showed in 1948 when he published his now-classic *Roman Ways in the Weald*.[1]

The literature about roads (little has been written about lanes and paths) is so voluminous that I do not propose to waste space, beyond a summary treatment, in rehearsing what is already common knowledge. Thus the fieldworker who wishes to study pre-Roman trackways in his neighbourhood may be referred for guidance as to the evidence and methods of discovery to Dr. G. B. Grundy's articles on the ancient trackways of various counties as published some years ago in the *Archaeological Journal*.[2]

Best of all, the beginner—who can be led wildly astray by some of the amateur stuff already in print—should read chapters 5, 6 and 7 of Crawford's *Archaeology in the Field* on Roman roads and earlier trackways. Crawford's views were character-

---

[1] Revised edition, 1965 (Phoenix House).
[2] For example, 'The Ancient Highways of Dorset, Somerset, and South-West England' in *Arch. Journal,* vols. XCIV and XCV (1934, 1935).

ized by a forthright commonsense. He always had his feet
firmly on the ground of human experience, and he was (in my
lay judgement) the greatest British archaeologist of his time.

The earliest trackways have been studied most intensively
in the limestone uplands of southern and eastern England.
Here the reader is referred to *Ancient Trackways of Wessex* by
H. W. Timperley and Edith Brill (1965) which also contains a
useful bibliography, and to Professor W. F. Grimes's essay on
'The Jurassic Way' in *Aspects of Archaeology in Britain and
Beyond* (1951). Another model study for fieldworkers in more
difficult terrain is Miss L. F. Chitty's essay on 'The Clun-Clee
Ridgeway: a Prehistoric Trackway across South Shropshire'
in *Culture and Environment: Essays in Honour of Sir Cyril Fox*
(1963).

Probably the best-known of all books about old roads is also
the most dangerous. This is the late Mr. Watkins's *The Old
Straight Track,* which should be read only by the most strong-
minded reader. As O. G. S. Crawford rightly says, the book
was 'based upon a mis-conception of primitive society, and
supported by no evidence. His writings on the subject are quite
valueless.'[1]

Prehistoric trackways may seem remote from modern life,
not even connected at all clearly with the beginnings of local
history; but they have in fact a very close bearing upon the
origins of many of our towns. So, to take a local example, there
can be little doubt that the beginnings of the town of Melton
Mowbray in Leicestershire must be sought at the crossing of
Eye valley by an Iron Age trackway running down from the
uplands to the south and rising on the farther side towards
the wooded hills of north Leicestershire. The age of the trackway can be safely put at Late Iron Age as it is clearly associated
with the hill-fort of Burrough Hill, four miles to the south of
Melton. It can be followed from the town first as a motor-road,
then as a cart-track, and finally as a footpath to the foot of the
hill-fort.

Where Melton now stands, ridges of high ground approached
the river (which floods heavily and rapidly in winter) so giving

[1] *Archaeology in the Field,* p. 75n.

the shortest possible crossing of the flood-plain. The site of Melton is similar to that of Stamford and the Welland crossing. At Melton the ground rises rapidly southward to some 90 ft. above the river; but on the northern side of the crossing it climbs quickly to a little plateau some 25 to 30 ft. above the river. It was on this flat ledge, safely above all winter flooding, that the Saxon market-place was established and a church built near by.[1]

Though no town grew up at this river crossing for some centuries (there is no evidence of Roman occupation here) there can be little doubt that some kind of early market, at first on a casual basis, grew up together with a sprinkling of huts long before anything was recognizable as a town. Two pagan Anglo-Saxon cemeteries, discovered on the outskirts of the present town, show that it was inhabited at least by the sixth century or the early seventh. And it was the Iron Age trackway that really determined the first crossing of the river and the site of the first huts.

At Exeter, in the far south-west of England, the present High Street is not only on a Roman line but is also identical with a trackway of Iron Age date running along the spine of a gravel ridge a hundred feet above the river. At Oxford the spine of the town—Cornmarket Street—began as a prehistoric trackway running north and south towards a ford over the Thames, again long before any town made its appearance on this site. Langport in Somerset, though not mentioned as a settlement until the early tenth century, owes its ultimate origin and its present elongated shape (hence 'the long port' of its name) to a prehistoric causeway which here crossed the flood-plain of the river Parrett at the narrowest point between two ridges of high ground.

ROMAN ROADS

'Our knowledge of Roman roads has now reached a point where the principal task in field work is filling up the outstand-

---

[1] A market is mentioned at Melton in a charter dated 1077 (Hunt, *Notes on Medieval Melton Mowbray* (Grantham, 1965).

ing gaps in the more important roads and dealing with the problem of minor local roads.' So says the Ordnance Survey in *Field Archaeology* (H.M.S.O., 4th edn., 1963). Field-workers should possess their own copy of this invaluable manual. Here, and in chapters 1 and 3 of Margary's *Roman Ways in the Weald,* they will find the necessary guidance as to what to look for and how to recognize it in the field. The introduction to the same writer's two-volume work on *Roman Roads in Britain* should also be digested for the same purpose.

The latest edition of the Ordnance Survey map of Roman Britain is now ten years old and the worker on Roman roads in a particular locality should consult the Archaeology Officer (Ordnance Survey, Chessington, Surrey) as to any additional information which has not yet reached the published map.

Since Mr. Margary's book on the Wealden roads the minor roads of Roman Britain have attracted increasing attention from local fieldworkers. In various parts of England one detects on the map what appear to be deliberately planned patterns of local roads the origin of which is still mysterious. The 2½-inch maps are the best for this preliminary inspection. These patterns are most likely to be Roman in date. They are highly localized and could be the surviving traces of *centuriation*.[1]

Mr. Margary describes one such grid-pattern at Ripe in Sussex (pages 204–7 of *Roman Ways in the Weald*) and concludes: 'Incredible as it may seem, we do appear to have in this area a survival of Roman land measurements too detailed to be by any possibility an accidental coincidence. . . . If we are compelled to regard the layout of this area as of Roman origin, then it follows that the lanes bounding the plots represent the 'occupation roads' of that period. No doubt they would be mere unmetalled farm tracks and it is not to be expected that remains of metalled Roman roads would be found there.'

[1] On this subject Margary gives a succinct account: 'It was customary in Roman times to establish State land settlement areas, often for time-expired soldiers or other settlers, which were laid out as a series of rectangles or squares, according to strict rules, and many such are still clearly traceable on the maps of Italy. They are also to be seen in the North African colonies, but had not hitherto been definitely proved to exist in Britain. The process is usually called 'centuriation,' because the land units of a plot were originally in multiples of a hundred.'

In the extreme north-west corner of Norfolk the one-inch map reveals a remarkable pattern of straight local roads, and the 2½-inch and 6-inch maps reinforce this impression. For about ten miles along the coast, from Holme-next-the-Sea to Brancaster (and perhaps beyond) this pattern is very marked. How far inland it extends is not yet certain, but it may go back as far as the straight road running from Ringstead through Choseley towards Burnham Market. On the west this pattern—which is pretty certainly Roman in origin—is bounded by Peddars Way, a known Roman road, and northwards it peters out towards the salt marshes along the shore.

This remarkable pattern, which divides up the landscape into square or rectangular blocks, is clearest of all in the most westerly coastal parish, that of Holme-next-the-Sea. Here Peddars Way terminated on the shore probably as the embarkation point for a ferry across *Metaris Aest* (The Wash) to the Lincolnshire shore near Burgh le Marsh.

Some of the original road pattern has perished, for the soils are light and sandy and any unmetalled occupation roads (as these mostly were) would tend to dissolve back into the ground unless kept in being in later centuries. Nevertheless, the vanished pieces remain on the map as straight hedge-lines and hence can be recovered. Moreover, there exists a map of Holme-next-the-Sea made in 1609 which shows more of the original lay-out than survives today (see Map VI).

Further points of interest emerge from the map and from the evidence of archaeological finds. The road known as Kirkgate in 1609 does not conform to the rectangular pattern but runs diagonally across an approximate square. Either it was a completely new road when the church was built (eleventh century?) or it was a modification of an original Roman road. Research could probably determine this debatable point. Secondly, the large rectangular blocks of land between the Hunstanton–Brancaster road on the north and the parish boundary to the south, here called Green Bank, show a remarkable uniformity of size: they are, from west to east, 207, 195, 212, and 202 acres respectively. The argument for a large-scale planned lay-out of holdings is considerably strengthened by this

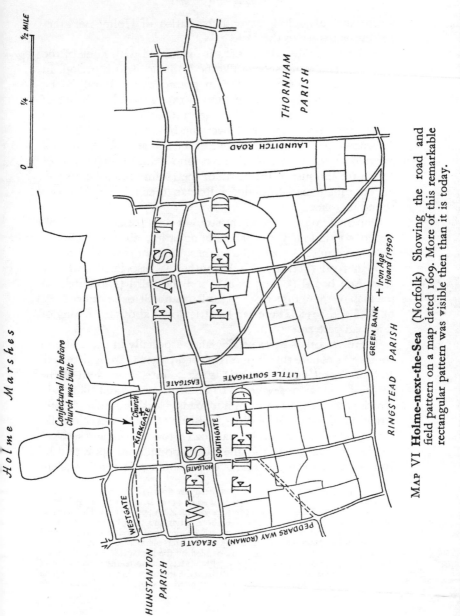

MAP VI **Holme-next-the-Sea** (Norfolk) Showing the road and field pattern on a map dated 1609. More of this remarkable rectangular pattern was visible then than it is today.

uniformity, extending beyond the parish of Holme-next-the-Sea into parishes to the east.[1]

Archaeologically, the pattern is associated with finds of the Iron Age and more specifically the Romano-British period. In 1861 some fragments of Roman pottery were found in the parish of Holme-next-the-Sea, and in 1950 a founder's hoard of Iron Age date was found alongside the Green Bank (surely a significant name, too). Just over the boundary of Holme, in Thornham parish and within one of the 200-acre blocks already referred to, there were finds of Romano-British pottery in 1948 and 1950; and just to the north of the Holme-Brancaster road, in Thornham parish again, a Roman cremation burial was found in 1940.

One final point: three of the straight roads of Holme are followed continuously by parish boundaries, always a sign of great antiquity in a road. One of these straight roads is a known Roman road (Peddars Way), another is associated with the Iron Age hoard (Green Bank), and the third (Launditch on the map of 1609) runs close to the Romano-British pottery finds of 1948 and 1950. There can be little doubt about the dating of this road-pattern.[2]

There are other parts of England, especially in the east and south-east, where this suggestive road-pattern can be detected. In Suffolk, for example, there is the country just south of the town of Bungay, represented by South Elmham and Ilketshall, which shows a pattern of minor roads, parish boundaries, and straight hedge-lines strongly reminiscent of north-west Norfolk. It is bisected by a known Roman road (Stone Street) and some of the lesser local roads and the parish boundaries appear to be laid out parallel to this road. South Elmham is a very ancient

[1] Dr. Gordon Ward appears to have been the first to draw attention to this road lay-out and the uniformity of at least some of the land-blocks, in 'A Roman Colony near Brancaster,' *Norfolk Archaeology,* vol. XXV, pp. 373–85. He set out in this article to show 'that the sites, the boundaries and the divisions of certain Roman soldier settlements in Britain can still be identified,' and he was convinced that the Holme-Brancaster pattern was one of such planned settlements.

[2] The fourth side, on the north, is bounded by the low water mark of the sea today and does not represent an original boundary owing to the reclamation of marshes subsequent to Roman times. Perhaps the sea-bank shown on the 2½-inch map represents the Roman boundary on the north as some of the planned roads run up to it and seem to be associated with it.

piece of country. It formerly comprised ten separate parishes (now there are six), was a deanery in itself, and the centre of the second diocese established in East Anglia. At South Elmham St. Cross are the ruins of the old Minster, almost certainly built in the 680s as the mother-church of this diocese.

Ilketshall is a Scandinavian name, derived from the personal name Ulfketill. But like Holme (which is a Scandinavian word for 'island') Ilketshall is a much older settlement than the Danish take-over of the year 879. Ulfketill simply took over a much older estate and gave it his name. The whole of the South Elmham-Ilketshall countryside would repay a microscopic examination on the map and on the ground, not forgetting the archaeological evidence where it exists.

CATTLE ROADS

The ultimate origins of many roads, other than the planned roads of the Roman period, are still obscure. Some may not have existed until villages were founded, when they were trodden out as inter-village paths; but there must have been many older trackways, trodden out in the first place perhaps by cattle, which determined the site of village-settlements rather than *vice versa*. Such roads may be detected by their winding course, winding that is for no apparent reason today, and by the fact that they keep along the margin between two different sorts of farming country. Above all, perhaps, this is true of country bordering upon marshland, like the winding road along the north coast of Norfolk, particularly between say Stiffkey and Weybourne (see chapter 10).

Another such area lies on the borders of Norfolk and Suffolk in the indeterminate and still marshy country where the Little Ouse and the Waveney rise within a few yards of each other to flow in opposite directions. Here, for example, a winding by-road called Low Road in one place and Fen Street in another waggles along just below the 100-foot contour from Diss towards Redgrave, and so westwards past Thelnetham and Hopton and back along the north side of the marshy valley through Blo Norton and Bressingham to Diss. In two places along this northern fringe the road is again called Fen Street. At many places along this winding cattle-road there are short straight tracks leading down to the marshes, what would be called 'go-downs' in the East, down which the cattle would be driven to their summer pastures. In Burma, so Colonel C. P. H. Wilson informs me, one gets such cattleways along the edges of the marshes and oxbows, the cattle being driven out for grazing from the villages every day and back at night. This must have been the pattern in parts of ancient England.

Another type of cattle-road altogether is the *Drove Road* which has never been systematically studied in this country though the drove roads of Wales and Scotland have each been the subject of books.[1]

For centuries Welsh cattle have been driven into England by long-recognized routes. As long ago as the mid-thirteenth century there was a well established droving industry from all parts of Wales to Gloucester market and even farther into England. In the depths of the English Midlands, on the borders of Warwickshire and Northamptonshire, is a long stretch of by-road called *Welsh Road*. This is obviously part of a great through-route for Welsh cattle, but how it reached Wormleighton in Warwickshire and where it goes beyond Northamptonshire no one seems to have worked out. It seems to be heading for Brackley, but where beyond that? Then there is a minor road today called Banbury Lane for miles, which finishes up at Banbury in North Oxfordshire. It can be traced by name as far as the outskirts of Northampton, and may have been the drove road by which cattle fattened in the rich pastures of the Nene and Welland valleys were driven down to Banbury market for sale and redistribution to the south of England.

Another drove-road in eastern England is discoverable from the 2½-inch map. It betrays its origin and purpose by its name—Bullock Road—a name given to a long stretch of lane which runs parallel with the A.1 in Huntingdonshire for about fifteen miles. In parts it is now metalled, in others only a green lane,

[1] For Wales, see P. G. Hughes, *Wales and the Drovers* (1943), and for Scotland, A. R. B. Haldane, *The Drove Roads of Scotland*. (1952). I understand that a book is now in preparation on the drove roads of northern England.

and in not a few places it dwindles to a mere footpath along the side of a field.[1]

The course of the Bullock Road can be clearly traced for many miles northwards from a point on the A.1 near Alconbury Hill, passing local places like Coldharbour Farm, Moonshine Gap, and Flittermere Pond (surely an ancient watering-place for cattle on the move?). It is followed by parish boundaries for a good deal of the way, and for one short stretch it marks the boundary between Huntingdonshire and Northamptonshire: sure evidence of its antiquity. The clear line of road peters out at Elton Furze (on A.605) but it almost certainly went on to cross the Nene (perhaps at Wans*ford* where the A.1 crosses today) and so on to the Welland crossing (probably at Stam*ford*). North of Stamford it links up clearly with another ancient drove road known as the Drift—again a significant name—or Sewstern Lane. Eventually it seems to reach the Trent valley near Newark.

The whole road from at least the Trent Valley southwards was a drove road by which cattle were driven up to the all-devouring London market; but it is perhaps older than London itself for it was a prehistoric trackway in places.

The drove roads, or driftways, usually run roughly parallel to main traffic roads. When roads were turnpiked[2] the drovers naturally avoided them, not only because of the tolls but because of the traffic also, and the necessity to find grass for their cattle on the plod. So any long and fairly direct stretches of minor road or lanes running more or less parallel to a turnpike road should be suspected as old drove roads. Especially is this true where the road or lane or green way is followed by parish boundaries.

Not all drove roads headed for London. Many converged on recognized cattle markets in the provinces. These more local drove roads may be worked out on the map and on the ground all over the uplands of northern England. There were huge

---

[1] I am indebted to Dr. Max Hooper, of the Nature Conservancy at Abbot's Ripton, for drawing my attention to this drove road.

[2] The first turnpike road was created by an Act of 1663 and related to the section of the Great North Road passing through Hertfordshire, Cambridgeshire and Huntingdonshire.

gathering-places to start with (as at Great Close on Malham Moor) at which thousands of cattle were assembled; and then followed the redistribution to the pastures and markets of the south. On the long roads south there were recognized 'stances' where the cattle could be halted and watered overnight. Near by was often an inn or cottage at which the drovers themselves were given sustenance. Some inn-signs remain as evidence of the droving business, but most have disappeared with the ending of the trade. A good book is waiting to be written on this subject, but it can only be done after much patient research into maps and documents.

Other road-patterns associated with cattle are to be found on the map, above all in connection with large ponds or *meres* in otherwise rather waterless country, and with common pastures shared by a number of places round their margin. A good example of such a pond is Ringmere, on the Breckland of south Norfolk. Surrounded by large open heaths, this mere is the meeting-place of no fewer than five parishes. The parish boundaries were drawn long ago so as to give each parish an approach to, and a share in, this valuable drinking-place. Here, and at Langmere near by, roads and tracks come in from all directions. And passing between the two meres is one of the best examples in East Anglia of a drove-road. It seems to begin (or end, as the case may be) at Blackdyke, on the edge of the Fens, and runs for some fourteen miles due east, passing just north of Brandon, over the sandy wastes of the Breckland to Fowlmere, the largest of the heathland meres (18 acres when full). Thence it runs past the other meres to join Peddars Way on Roudham Heath. It may have continued to East Harling but its further course is unknown.[1]

Certain roads from prehistoric times onwards converged over long distances on extensive pastures common to a whole region. I have discussed some of these great 'regional pastures' in the first chapter of *The Common Lands of England and Wales*.[2]

---

[1] See R. Rainbird Clarke, *In Breckland Wilds* (1937), esp. Ch. V and pp. 68–70. O. G. S. Crawford, in *Archaeology in the Field* (1953) also has a useful chapter on Ponds, especially in Wessex.

[2] W. G. Hoskins and L. Dudley Stamp, *The Common Lands of England and Wales*. (Collins, 1963).

Among them were the whole of what later became the New Forest, the whole of Dartmoor and possibly the whole of central Somerset (the Levels). In south-eastern England *Andred's Weald,* or part of it, was common to the whole of Kent just as Dartmoor was common to the whole of what later became Devon.

The granite upland of Dartmoor was used as summer pasturage from neolithic times onwards. Well into historic times the farmers of Devon drove their cattle and sheep up to the Moor from over a wide area. When we realize this, the meaning of several long ridge-ways, followed by parish boundaries for many miles and heading for Dartmoor, becomes apparent. These ancient trackways, mostly in active use to this day can best be seen in the countryside to the south and north of the Moor. On the south side a number of ridgeways run from the coast up to the moorland edges. Such, for example, are the roads that start on the coast at Dartmouth, Strete, Slapton, Kingston, and Newton Ferrers.

To the north of the Moor there are similar long through-roads, the one most clearly evidenced on the map being that which follows the top of the high ground between the Taw and Torridge valleys, running through Winkleigh and thence due south to the Moor near Cawsand Beacon. The huge rounded hill of Cawsand—or Cosdon, to give it its proper name—is visible all the way from North Devon and guided the herdsmen for twenty miles or more.

Smaller uplands like the Clee Hills of south Shropshire, which afforded common pasture for a wide area around, had their local driftroads, now deeply sunken with age, converging upon them from prehistoric times. One such road, running up from Ludlow to the top of Brown Clee Hill, is still called The Thrift.

OTHER ROADS AND LANES

Some roads originated, as we have seen, as cattle-paths, especially where marshland fringed higher ground, or as paths and tracks leading to prehistoric ponds and pastures. Many other minor roads and lanes originated later, some as paths from one village to the next and others—perhaps more difficult to detect—as double-ditched boundaries of pre-Conquest estates and as boundaries to isolated farms settled in the same period.[1] Most of these boundary-roads and lanes can be satisfactorily elucidated with the aid of suitable maps and a scrutiny of the ground itself. Farm-boundaries in old-enclosed country are best discovered, to begin with, on the tithe maps of the 1840s and thereabouts. One must always bear in mind the possibility that the boundaries of farms do not invariably remain static, especially if the farms are part of a larger estate with an improving landlord. Estate maps of the sixteenth to eighteenth centuries, if they exist, may help to determine the older boundaries where there have been changes. But where the map shows that roads and lanes form the boundaries, it is likely that these represent aboriginal boundaries and that they are worth inspection on the ground.

Roads of later construction such as new pieces of turnpike road or those made as a result of parliamentary enclosure awards in the same period (roughly 1750–1850) are usually easily identified from contemporary maps and plans in county record offices and do not involve much if anything in the way of fieldwork. To this extent they may not attract much attention but those field-workers who are engaged in tracing Roman roads in their district should consult all these later records in order to ensure that a straight stretch of minor road which they suspect to be Roman was not in fact laid out by the enclosure commissioners at a much later date.

Similarly, the field-worker should be on his guard over diversions of roads. The commonest cause of such diversions in old roads was the making of gentlemen's parks in the eighteenth century, and sometimes earlier and later than this. Such diversions are often quickly suspected on examining the Ordnance map but they should nevertheless be checked wherever

---

[1] For such 'hollow ways' formed by double-ditching, see my *Making of the English Landscape* (1955), pp. 28, 56; and for the antiquity of the single farmsteads in south-west England see my chapter on 'The Highland Zone in Domesday Book' in *Provincial England* (1963). Most of these early farms had such boundaries where there was no natural boundary such as a stream.

possible from the estate records. More recent diversions can be tracked down in county council records, and some in earlier Quarter Sessions records. A special class of record relates to highway closure and diversion.[1] Often, too, the existence of an old bridge, now apparently leading nowhere in particular, will afford a valuable clue to a medieval or Tudor road which was later abandoned. The printed volumes of *Miscellaneous Inquisitions,* covering the period from Henry III to Richard II, also contain useful references to medieval roads and bridges and to now-abandoned traffic routes.

---

[1] See, for example, *Guide to the Kent County Archives Office* (1958), p. 26. An Act in 1697 'established the practice of examining proposed closure of highways by the process of a writ of *ad quod damnum* and an inquisition thereupon with the right of appeal to Quarter Sessions.' These records are usually accompanied by maps indicating the old and the new roads.

Two Tours

In this chapter I shall be concerned with two tours—one along a short stretch of the north Norfolk coast, the other across the middle of Somerset—not as a detailed exposition of local topography but in order to illustrate the variety of problems which arise when a particular piece of countryside is looked at in a certain way.

SOME FIELDWORK IN NORFOLK

About the middle of the cold grey coast of northern Norfolk is a stretch of country where the salt marshes fringe the sea, separated from it only by a shingle ridge. The sea-margin from Hunstanton to Weybourne has been described as 'the finest example of coastal marshes in these islands.' They are not only of the greatest interest to the botanist, the physical geographer, and the ornithologist, but not less to the local historian and topographer. To illustrate what I mean I propose to take a small stretch, between four and five miles in length, beginning at Cley-next-the-Sea and running eastwards to where the low cliffs begin at Weybourne.

Cley, an attractive little decayed sea-port and fishing-village, lies on the eastern side of the former estuary of the river Glaven. This estuary once ran up almost to the mill at Gland-ford; and a little above this point was the earliest safe crossing under natural conditions. The former extent of the estuary is

clearly seen on the 2½-inch map (sheet TG 04) by the area coloured to indicate the flood-plain today. Wiveton, on the western
side of the estuary, was also a sea-port as late as the early
seventeenth century. As late as 1823 the tide flowed up the
Glaven as far as Glandford; so the Saxon ford that gave the
place its name lay immediately above the tidal limit.

The first thing one notices about Cley is the position of the
splendid parish church, more than half a mile from the village,
overlooking a large green. An ancient church standing by
itself like this almost invariably denotes that the settlement
which it served has moved away at some date. This is known to
have happened at Cley because of the fortunate survival of an
Elizabethan map (1586) which reveals that at that date most of
the village lay round the church. So the first topographical
problem emerges at once—the date at which the village moved
northwards nearer the sea, and the reasons for the migration.
In all probability the migration was connected with the taking-
in of the salt marshes by the Dutch drainage engineer van
Hasedunck and others along this coast in the 1630s and 1640s.
Calthorpe's Bank at Cley was constructed in 1627. This allowed
ships to use Cley quay but obstructed navigation up to Wiveton. A return of shipping in 1582 shows that Wiveton possessed
several ships of 100 tons and over, the Blakeney and Cley ships
being generally smaller.[1] The natural opposition of Wiveton
to the destruction of its coastal and other trade led to the demoli-
tion of Calthorpe's Bank, but Cley marshes were finally em-
banked and reclaimed about 1650. The topography of this
piece of coast is much more complicated than these simple
events would suggest, but we are only concerned with it here
for its effect on the settlement at Cley, which, as the tide was
pushed farther back, so to speak, migrated from its original
position round the church to a point considerably nearer the
sea.

Yet even this is not the whole story, for the traveller cannot

---

[1] For details of this coastline and some of its history see J. A. Steers, *The
Coastline of England and Wales* (2nd edn, 1964), pp. 352–4 and 368–9. Steers's
account is based on the pioneer work of B. Cozens-Hardy, *Trans. Norfolk and
Norwich Nat. Hist. Society,* vol. 12, (1924–9).

fail to notice that there are bridges across the old estuary at both Cley and Wiveton. That at Wiveton is, indeed, a well-preserved medieval bridge, probably of fifteenth-century date. It has a total span of twelve yards, with a width between its parapets of twelve feet, and consists of a single pointed arch with five chamfered ribs. It appears to be the bridge referred to in the will of Robert Paston of Wiveton, dated 1482, in which he leaves 6d to the repair of the chapel of the Holy Trinity *super pontem*. No chapel now exists. Wiveton Bridge did not interfere with the navigation of the Glaven to the quay at Wiveton, which lay somewhere to the north and could probably be traced today by the assiduous field-worker. But an earlier record considerably complicates the whole matter. As is so often the case, history would be much easier to write if one had only one record; additional records only complicate what might have been a simple account. But the local historian is used to this difficulty and indeed welcomes it, for it throws up problems to be solved.

This earlier record is a Miscellaneous Inquisition, a class of record which has already been referred to (Chapter 3) as one that is invaluable for the local historian and topographer. It relates to an inquiry held at Holt, the nearest market-town, on the Saturday before the Feast of St. Margaret in the year 1380.[1] Eighteen men of the neighbourhood met on a July morning—it was Holt market-day, a convenient day for assembling such a jury—to inquire about 'two ancient bridges in Cley and Wiveton now broken down and almost impassable . . . to discover who built them and who is bound to repair them (and) whether the road over them is the king's highway of ancient use or a newly begun path. . . .'

The jury reported that a stone bridge in Wiveton and a wooden bridge in Cley and Wiveton 'across certain brooks which go down to the sea in those towns' were so broken that men can hardly cross them. There had been no bridge here in or before the twentieth year of the reign of Edward I (i.e. 1291–2) but only a path by which men crossed at their own peril after the ebb of the sea. This was never the king's highway which, so

[1] *Cal. Misc. Inqns.* Vol. IV, no. 124 (pp. 76–7).

the jury said, ran through the middle of the town of Glandford, two miles (*stadia*) to the south.[1]

They then go on to say that William Storm, father of Thomas Storm of Snitterley (the old name of Blakeney), who is still alive, of his devotion and alms built the two bridges in the same path for the soul of Hugh his father and with the said Hugh's goods. No individual contributed thereto nor the commonalty of Wiveton or any adjoining villages; nor were they accustomed from ancient times or bound in law to do so. If the bridges were not to be repaired in future, it would not be to anybody's damage, because no one is bound to repair them and the highway is so near. The stone bridge could be repaired for twenty marks and the wooden bridge for twenty shillings.

The jury were evidently anxious not to place the burden of repairing the bridges on any of their own villages and townships and pointed out that it was not far in any event to the old crossing at Glandford. Nevertheless, the bridges were repaired or rebuilt not long afterwards, to judge by the date of the surviving bridge at Wiveton. The map of 1586 shows the two bridges on the same road, one of one arch to the east, the other of two arches to the west. This record seems to show that both the bridges were near Wiveton, and that there was no bridge at Cley where the present one stands. If there had been, ships could not have reached the quay at Wiveton in the sixteenth century, as they did; and the record clearly says that the bridges had been built 'in the same path', presumably crossing over two channels of the Glaven at this point. The estuary must already have silted up below Glandford for such a bridge to have been possible; and judging by the evidence of the record it was first constructed about the middle of the fourteenth century as the son of the builder was still alive in 1380. The date could be ascertained more precisely if we could discover the date of Hugh Storm's death. The object of making these bridges is clear if one looks at the large-scale maps. They afforded a short

[1] The distance is nothing like two miles, but the line of the medieval king's highway is very evident on the 2½-inch map. Ancient lanes—their antiquity is evidenced by the fact that parish boundaries run along them—approach the ford at Glandford from both east and west.

cut from the growing port of Blakeney, where Hugh Storm lived (probably as a merchant) to the central market-town of Holt, cutting out the long detour by Glandford where there was in any event no bridge, but a shallow ford.[1]

Two other topographical problems remain to be mentioned at Cley before we leave it for the coast-road to Salthouse. Where was the medieval quay at Cley before the village migrated to its present position? And is the small-scale street-plan of post-Elizabethan Cley a miniature of the rows at Yarmouth? As to the first question one can only point to a considerable depression immediately south of the medieval church which could well have been an inlet or small harbour under natural conditions. Even on the 2½-inch map this inlet is clearly indicated by the indentation of the 25-foot contour at this point. Excavation might produce an answer in the shape of the remains of a stone quay or of other buildings suggesting the presence of a harbour.

As to the second question, no firm answer can readily be given. A detailed study of the street-pattern, with the aid of old maps, might well produce some light.

It is now time to leave Cley and to walk eastwards along the coastal road to Salthouse. This road follows a winding course at the junction of the old salt marshes and the arable slopes, just high enough above the marshes to be safe from all the inundations of the sea except such tremendous break-throughs as those of the winters of 1287 and 1953. It is known as The Skirts in places, which suitably describes its course. Just east of Cley, Romano-British pottery was found in 1924 and two miles farther on other Romano-British pottery was found in 1851, beside the former course of this ancient road.[2] Such a winding road at the junction of arable and marshland is almost certainly a prehistoric (Iron Age) cattle track of the type described in Chapter 9, and the pottery finds help to give it a date. It must have been in regular use before the Romano-British population

[1] There is still only a foot-bridge at Glandford, and larger traffic must go round by Cley or Wiveton bridges.
[2] The modern road deviates from the original line just east of Salthouse village to climb the side of Warborough Hill and then to take a safer course some way inland. The old road continued along what is now called Meadow Lane.

left their pottery alongside it. At Gramborough Hill, a green island between the marsh and the shingle beach, Roman bricks and pottery have been found in considerable quantities, though none (unfortunately) was ever preserved for expert inspection.

The place-name Salthouse next engages our attention. It means what it implies—'house for storing salt'—and is so recorded in Domesday Book. Were there salt-pans here in late Saxon times, and should the field-worker look for those hills of waste material that characterise coastal districts where salt was made over a long period of time? The best of these sites are found along the Essex shore of the Thames Estuary—the so-called Red Hills—and along the Lincolnshire coast, above all at Ingoldmells Point to the north of Skegness and not far across the water from the north coast of Norfolk.

'The precise method of making salt from the sea varies over the world with climatic conditions, and it is evident that no reliance could be placed on natural evaporation in open salt-pans in Britain. The methods used in Britain are all basically concerned with boiling down salt-enriched water and casting the resulting salt into blocks of standard sizes and weights. A large variety of specialized clay receptacles and accessories were used, all of which were cheaply made and readily expendable. Thus the salters' working places are often marked by low but extensive mounds of earth reddened by fire (red hills). While they are chiefly made of soil they also contain many broken clay objects, chief among which in Britain is the 'handbrick', a rough column of fired clay squeezed up in the hand and flattened at both ends. These were used in great numbers to support clay troughs of different shapes over fires, and there are other objects like moulds for casting the salt into blocks and square-sectioned clay bats tapering towards the ends. The broken remains of all these, along with clay partitions for the troughs and various clay squeezes of different forms used as supports and spacing pieces add up, with much burnt earth and ash, to make a Red Hill. The date of any site will be determined by the associated pottery and other domestic rubbish left behind by the salt-makers, whose work seems to have been seasonal.' (*Field Archaeology*, 4th edn. 1963, p. 80.)

With this description in mind, the neighbourhood of Salt-house raises some interesting questions. On the modern 2½-inch map the name 'Sarbury Hill' occurs immediately west of the village; but on a map of 1649 it is called 'Salt Hill', and the question arises whether this low hill is the debris of early salt-making activities. Similarly, the Roman 'bricks and pottery' found on Gramborough Hill (which is 'Greenborough' on the 1649 map) may well represent the debris of salt-makers. Indeed, one wonders whether all the hills along the very edge of the sea known today as Cley Eye, Little Eye, Flat Eye (now nearly eroded by the sea), and Gramborough are not all 'salt hills'. Only excavation could prove this. They may be natural moraines formed in the last Ice Age, but the archaeological evidence is very suggestive, as is the 'Salt Hill' of 1649. Half-way between Cley and Salthouse are other small hills beside the coastal road known as Walsey Hills. In default of any early forms of this name, it is impossible to suggest a meaning for 'Walsey'; but again excavation would decide whether they are a natural glacial formation or artificial heaps of debris from salt-making.[1]

In doing fieldwork along this coast one must remember that coastal erosion, and major changes in relative sea and land levels (such as occurred in the late thirteenth century and at other times), have removed a great deal of evidence. Thus it has been calculated that the main beach of Salthouse was eroded land-wards by some 275 yards between 1649 and 1924, at an average rate of about a yard a year. At this rate the coastline of say the year 1500 would have been about a quarter of a mile farther to the north than it is today. Half of Gramborough Hill, with whatever evidence it once contained, is now under the sea, and so all along this piece of coast.

These coastal changes have had their impact in other ways. Thus the fifteenth-century western tower of Blakeney church is matched by a miniature tower of the same period at the N.E. end, probably in order to give a navigational 'fix' by getting the

For valuable historical and archaeological surveys of salt-making on the Lincolnshire coast and marshland from the Iron Age down to the early seventeenth century, see *Lincolnshire Architectural and Archaeological Society Reports and Papers,* Vol. 8 New Series (1960).

two towers in line. Similarly, in the N.W. corner of the church-
yard at Salthouse are the ruins of a medieval chapel. But why
should there be a detached chapel in a churchyard like this? Was
this also a navigational fix, i.e. to get the lofty tower of Salthouse church and the little chapel in line? And if so, did the two
fixes at Blakeney and Salthouse indicate some critical approach
to a harbour along this dangerous coast in the fifteenth century?

Behind Salthouse, rising some two hundred feet above sea-
level, are the heathlands, criss-crossed with many ancient roads
(as indicated by parish boundaries and other evidence) and
dotted with Bronze Age barrows. All these old roads and lanes
would repay plotting on the map and exploration on the
ground. Salthouse Heath almost resembles a prehistoric Clap-
ham Junction. To look at only one of these tracks, running due
south from Salthouse, it may well have been the salt-road from
the Saxon salt-warehouse on the marsh-edge to the royal manor
of Holt which belonged to Edward the Confessor and had
possibly been a royal estate for long before that.

In Domesday Book, the royal manor of Holt included Cley
and Blakeney (then called Snitterley) as outlying estates. This
probably represents the fragments of a once-large royal
estate along this coast and stretching some miles inland; and
there is some reason to suppose that the parishes of Salthouse
and Kelling once formed part of this large estate. Thus it is
clear from the map that the boundaries of the two parishes fit
together in a way that shows they were once a single unit; and
various medieval records show that they had some ancient
connexion.

Kelling is an ancient place-name, indicating settlement (like
Sheringham, not so far away) by an early folk, in this case
'Cylla's people'. This early settlement was placed, as usual,
some distance inland from the shore. How far inland we cannot
say because of the coastal changes already referred to, but even
today Kelling church is 1½ miles from the beach and was perhaps two miles inland when it was first built. Subsequently, but
well back in Saxon times, a small settlement grew up on the edge
of the salt marshes where salt-makers worked and saw to the
storage and distribution of salt at the 'salt house'. In time, this

coastal settlement grew large enough to have its own church, and a new ecclesiastical parish of Salthouse was carved out of the original Kelling.

Such a large storehouse for salt is known to have existed at Bitterne, on a big bend in the Itchen estuary in Hampshire. Bitterne is derived from *byht*, 'a bend', and *aern* 'storehouse'. That this was a storehouse for salt made locally along the estuary is strongly suggested by a reference in a Winchester pipe roll dated 1207–8 which shows that salt was being sent from here to other manors of the bishop of Winchester at Downton, Farnham, and Sutton. In the same way Salthouse on the Norfolk coast must have been a central warehouse for the collection and distribution of salt, perhaps from as far away as the Lincolnshire coast round Ingoldmells and from the salt-pans recorded at Burnham in Domesday Book.[1]

In Kelling itself there are various places of interest to the field-worker. Warborough Hill, with a steep face to the sea, derives its name from the Old English *Waru-beorg*, 'a watch-hill' and was evidently a look-out and perhaps a beacon before the Norman conquest. Off Weybourne, deep water comes nearer to the shore than anywhere along the coast of Norfolk. As a consequence Weybourne Hope, on the shore, has always been regarded as a particular dangerpoint for England when invasion is threatened. Warborough Hill watched the sea-approaches to this danger-point.

Traces of the hurried fortifications of 1588 can be discovered along the low cliffs here with the aid of a contemporary map preserved at Hatfield and published in *Norfolk Archaeology*. And all around lie the equally hurried defences of 1940, when Weybourne was rightly regarded as a possible landing-place for the mighty German invasion that was then awaited. Three lines of defences can still be seen: the sea-battered pill-boxes on the beach, the concrete emplacements on the low cliffs, and the last

[1] For Bitterne, see O. G. S. Crawford, 'Bitterne after the Romans', *Proc. Hampshire Field Club*, Vol. XVI (1944), pp. 148–55. Similarly, Arne in Dorset—standing on a large spur projecting into Poole Harbour—may well have derived its name from a storehouse for salt destined for the royal manor and borough of Wareham. Like Salthouse, it would have been a secondary settlement from an older one, in this case from Wareham.

line of defence on the seaward edge of the heathland behind. These unsightly remains are as much a part of English history as the fragments that survive from the year 1588.

Much Romano-British material—pottery and gold coins—has come out of the low cliff immediately west of Weybourne Hope. The sea has washed away most of this site, and one can only speculate fruitlessly what kind of site it was originally.

Lastly, in this short tour, there is the massive Kelling Ditch —so called on a large-scale map of Weybourne made in 1704— which divided Weybourne from Kelling. It can be best seen between the Holt-Cromer road and Hundred-Acre Wood. It was evidently a prominent boundary to have this name perpetuated and could well have marked the division between the territory of Cylla's people (Kelling) and that of Scira's people (Sheringham). This is on the assumption that Weybourne was a secondary settlement from Sheringham, and the way the parish boundaries of Weybourne run would certainly suggest this original unity. In that event the fieldworker has on the Kelling-Weybourne boundary a great boundary ditch constructed in all probability in the fifth century or at the latest in the early sixth. And at this point we must bring our short exploration of the north Norfolk coast to an end for the time being.

SOME FIELDWORK IN SOMERSET

As the diesel train makes it way down from Castle Cary, heading westwards, a massive block of limestone upland—a plateau mostly some 200 to 250 ft. above sea-level—appears ahead. The upland is crowned by a compact little town built of a pale-blue limestone from the Lower Lias, its roofs covered with bright red pantiles. This is Somerton, the ancient capital of Somerset, a town that is as attractive to study at close range as the distant view of it promises. 'The market-place of Somerton is one of the most happily grouped urban pictures in Somerset' (Pevsner); and it is here that we begin our exploration of mid-Somerset, westwards as far as the town of Bridgwater. Once again, I am not trying to describe all that can be seen in this most beautiful and rewarding of English counties, but

merely indicating as we go along some of the things that call
for fieldwork, for more detailed exploration on the ground and
in the documents.

Somerton is only one of many places on this fascinating
plateau that calls for microscopic study. From Langport, on its
western edge, to Kingsdon on the eastern slopes, this piece of
country is full of topographical problems for the field-worker
possessed of local knowledge and a seeing eye. The upland
contains one of the richest concentrations of Romano-British
settlement and farming in Britain.[1] It was a favoured corner—
'the fashionable preserve of gentleman farmers, as the great
villas with their ostentatious bathing-suites demonstrate'
(Pevsner). High, dry, fertile, and blessed with a softer climate
than most of Britain could supply, this island rising from the
marshes of the Cary and the Parrett attracted rich farmers from
the Roman period onwards.

In Saxon times it formed a huge royal estate centred upon
Somerton, which stretched all the way from Langport to
Kingsdon. No charter survives to tell us the boundaries of this
estate, as so many do for Somerset[2] but the lanes around the
foot of Bradley Hill, more especially that round the northern
and north-western sides, look to me (on the ground) very like
the massive boundary banks of Saxon date that I have seen
elsewhere in south-western England. Indeed, the whole of the
minor road along the northern foot of the upland as far as
Pitney might well be studied as possibly the original boundary
of the royal estate between the dry upland and the vast undrained
marshes of that date. Such a boundary would probably be of
seventh-century date when the Saxons overran this part of
Somerset and their royal house appropriated the best lands for
themselves as we know they did in Devon;[3] and I suspect it ran
all around the upland if one could trace it.

[1] See the map in *Proc. Somerset A. and N. H. Soc.* (1951) Vol. XCVI, p. 45.
[2] See G. B. Grundy, *The Saxon Charters and Field Names of Somerset*, published
in 1935 by the Somersetshire Archaeological and Natural History Society; and
also H. P. R. Finberg, *The Early Charters of Wessex* (Leicester University Press,
1964), pp. 109–54. Though Dr. Grundy worked out many of the boundaries of
the Somerset charters, the local field-worker is advised to go over them again on
the ground. Not all scholars accept all his identifications.
[3] See W. G. Hoskins, *Provincial England*, p. 29.

Langport was still a part of Somerton as late as 1086, and at the other end of the upland we have Kingsdon, which means 'the royal hill-pasture' as distinct from the summer pastures of the river-marshes. So the royal estate was still largely intact at the end of the eleventh century, though Huish (Episcopi) had been granted away to the bishop of Wells somewhat earlier.

Domesday Book, which is so detailed and informative for south-western England, says of Langport: 'there is a borough called Lanporth in which dwell 34 burgesses, paying 15 shillings. And there are two fisheries paying 10 shillings.' Langport first occurs as a name in the Burghal Hidage (early tenth century) as one of the *burhs* or fortresses set up by Alfred in the late ninth century against the Danes. This earthwork was apparently on the lip of the hill, near the present church, at the top of the town. It was obviously intended to guard the vital river crossing over the Parrett, a river that was navigable to this point until within living memory.

Langport lay along an ancient road or trackway—possibly prehistoric in origin—which dropped down the hillside from the Somerton upland and made the shortest crossing of the Parrett marshes for many miles up or down river. This road became in Saxon times the main traffic route from Somerton to Taunton. The name *Portway* just across the river from Langport, indicates its ancient purpose, as a road between market-towns.

Langport means 'the long *port* or market town'. Its shape is seen in a beautiful profile from the Western Region railway and is particularly revealing when the winter floods are out and lapping round the foot of the hill, leaving the little town high and dry. This shape was dictated by the site, the town growing house by house down the narrow roadway from the hilltop *burh* to the edge of the flood-plain. By the early tenth century it was sufficiently important and secure to permit the establishment of a mint; the earliest surviving coin from the Langport mint is *c.* 930. By the end of the eleventh century it had, as we saw above, 34 burgesses, whose houses (or the sites thereof) must be sought in the upper part of the town.

But there were almost certainly other families not regarded as burgesses and not noticed by Domesday, whose huts pro-

MAP VII **Langport** (Somerset) An Anglo-Saxon *burh*
of burgages below the hill, still almost unchange
the first edition of the 25-inch map surveyed

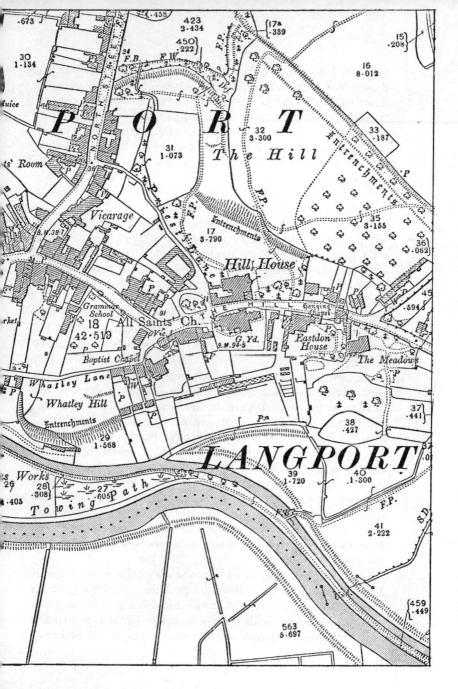

...in, but showing also a well-developed medieval pattern
...produced by permission from the Ordnance Survey from
... and revised in 1902.)

bably lay further down the street and nearer the river. Many of these families must have been engaged in the two valuable fisheries mentioned in Domesday. Thus, if one had the opportunity of excavating along the main street of Langport one ought to find the foundations at least of more or less substantial late Saxon houses in the upper part of the town, and the traces of miserable huts in the lower part, if they survive at all—if only as post-holes.

Such a statement about the population of English towns in the late eleventh century affects our entire notion of the size of towns at that period and hence their archaeology, particularly of house sites. The basic authority for making this assertion is the remarkable entry for Dunwich in Suffolk, where Domesday tells us there were 236 burgesses 'and 180 poor men less two', not to mention 80 other men who render £4 and 8,000 herrings and who were evidently poor fishermen.

It is inconceivable that no other borough in England housed any 'poor men' or non-burgesses. Domesday simply disregarded them as financially valueless; though economically they formed a very important social group for from their ranks most of the labouring class was drawn. There has never been any proper discussion of the non-burgess element in the Domesday population. Perhaps the best summary of the difficulties is to be found in Carl Stephenson, *Borough and Town: a Study of Urban Origins in England* (1933), pp. 79–81. This is not just an academic issue for the student of urban topography since it affects the archaeology of the whole site. It is clear to me that in excavating towns of this period (Late Saxon-Early Norman) one must expect to find considerable areas, whole streets in the larger towns, which contain nothing but working-class huts of the most miserable construction and yielding little or nothing in the way of 'finds' save perhaps a few pieces of poor pottery.

One other point needs to be made about the topography of Langport and that is that since the road along which it grew up was probably of prehistoric origin the lower part of the town may well have been built upon a causeway of the type that has been increasingly recognized in recent years in the Somerset

Levels, notably around Shapwick on the north side of the Poldens and not many miles from Langport.[1] The crossing of the Parrett marshes at this critical point must be of vast antiquity.

The winding road from Langport to Aller bears all the marks of an ancient cattle-track following the contour just above the edge of the marshes. A mile or so north of Aller it turns westward across the marshes (perhaps another ancient causeway?) to reach the first of an interesting group of four villages, all sited on slight eminences above the Levels. Geologically, they lie upon the Burtle Beds,[2] which gives them a dry foundation for building, raised above the annual winter floods. These villages are Othery, Middlezoy, Weston Zoyland and Chedzoy.

The greater part of this territory, apart from the dry islands on which the villages stood, was marshland: deeply flooded for perhaps half the year, drying out for summer pasturage for the other half. All of this piece of country (except Chedzoy) was included in an enormous grant by Ine, king of the West Saxons, to Glastonbury Abbey as far back as the year 725. It was then known by the single name of *Sowy*, containing (so says Ekwall) a stream-name plus the Old English word for 'an island'. This island stands out clearly on the geological map, being entirely defined by the Burtle Beds.

Chedzoy, on a separate island, has a different derivation. It goes back to *Chedesie* (in a charter of 729) and means 'Cedd's island'. The present name has been influenced by the proximity of Weston Zoyland and Middlezoy.

The boundaries of the enormous grant of 725 start with the phrase: 'first from Wilbrittis-pathe to the middle of the river Parrett'. This path has been identified with the minor road running from Othery to the tiny hamlet of Pathe (so named to this day). It may well have originated then as a boundary between the island and the marsh now called North Moor; and

---

[1] See, for examples, H. Godwin, 'Prehistoric wooden trackways of the Somerset levels. . . .' *Proc. Prehistoric Society* (1960), Vol. XXVI, pp. 1–36.

[2] These are sandy deposits largely composed of comminuted shell and therefore easily drained. They determined the pattern of settlement over a large area of the Levels, and are named after the district of Burtle which lay between the Polden Hills and the marshes of the river Brue.

the boundary continued from Pathe along a small stream to the Parrett almost opposite Stathe.

Othery means 'other island'. It is not recorded before the year 1225 (in an Assize Roll), but it certainly existed long before that and formed part of the Glastonbury estate of *Sowy*. The fact that we have *Weston* Zoyland, *Middle*zoy, and Othery strongly suggests that Othery is a late name and that it probably replaced another Zoy name.

In Domesday Book we read under the heading of the lands of St. Mary of Glastonbury: 'the church itself[1] holds *Sowi*. Alnod the abbot held in the time of King Edward and it paid geld for 12 hides'. This is the same hidage as the grant of 725. The estate had been valued at £10 a year in 1066, but twenty years later its annual value had risen to £24. This remarkable increase in value of the lands now represented by the parishes of Weston Zoyland, Middlezoy, and Othery shows that the abbey was actively at work reclaiming the marshland by constructing a network of drainage ditches. Here then is a splendid opportunity for fieldwork, for many of the ditches or *rhines* (as they are locally termed) in this area must be precisely dateable to the years 1066–86. Some may indeed be even older as there is evidence from elsewhere in the Somerset Levels that Glastonbury Abbey was engaged in reclamation of the marshland as far back as the mid-tenth century. Looking at the ordnance map I would suggest that this early reclamation (tenth–eleventh centuries) is evidenced in the levels between the island of Sowy and the Parrett. The whole pattern made by the ditches, tracks, and minor roads in the area now called South Moor, Weston Level, and Earlake Moor is highly suggestive; but the fieldworker must not guess at these things. This is merely 'a hunch' derived from an inspection of the map, and detailed documentary research is required to link specific references in the medieval records to particular ditches, lanes, and other features. There may have been some early reclamation in the northern levels towards Sedgemoor: Langacre and Burdenham sound like early names; but in the main the northern

[1] i.e. the abbey retained this estate in its own hands and had not let it to a tenant, as was so often done on these large estates.

levels beyond Sowy waited for the major drainage schemes of the nineteenth century.

We can detect from the pages of Domesday Book what was happening immediately after the Norman Conquest. Perhaps the most important clue is the appearance of one *Girard Fossarius* as a substantial tenant of Glastonbury Abbey. He was 'Girard the ditch-maker', or more appropriately 'Girard the drainage-engineer'. He held the manor of Greinton, on the northern edge of Sedgemoor as a tenant of the abbey, and also a smaller estate of three virgates at Ham (probably Low Ham). Possibly Girard had been brought in by the first Norman abbot Thurstin, who was appointed in 1082, to undertake a large-scale drainage programme. If so, the rise in value of the Glastonbury marshland manors was even more spectacular than Domesday would suggest.

At Ham the rise in value was from £4 to £10; at Butleigh from £3 to £10; at Pilton £16 to £24; at Glastonbury itself the value of the manor had been doubled (£10 to £20); and at Brent Marsh there was an even more astonishing increase. It was worth £50 a year in 1086: 'when the abbot received it only £15'. These must be the marshes all around the foot of Brent Knoll. Here too is a piece of country that would repay detailed fieldwork, especially as so many of the necessary documents (e.g. medieval surveys and rentals of the Glastonbury estate) have been put into print.

The greater part of the Somerset Levels was in ecclesiastical hands by the eleventh century and earlier, and the records of the abbeys of Glastonbury, Muchelney, and Athelney, and those of the Dean and Chapter and Bishop of Wells, form a splendid start for the field-worker in this part of England. The Glastonbury records show large-scale reclamation and enclosure still going on round 'Sowy' in the first generation of the thirteenth century. A list made in 1238 shows, for example, that the abbot had recently created eighty holdings, representing some 250 acres or so of former wet moor, at a rent of fourpence an acre. So in the parishes of Weston Zoyland, Middlezoy and Othery, we have to trace on the ground the pattern of a landscape created at a varying pace between the early eighth century when the villages were probably first settled and the early sixteenth when the abbey finally lost its vast possessions.

One final remark about these 'Zoy' villages. The fine Perpendicular church of Weston Zoyland was largely rebuilt in the late fifteenth century and the early sixteenth. On one of the transept buttresses are the initials of Richard Bere, abbot of Glastonbury from 1493–1524, who evidently carried through this great work. The same initials occur on the south porch at Chedzoy, which was also largely reconstructed in the same generation. The church at Middlezoy, too, was largely remodelled at the same date, but here the abbot's initials do not appear, or at least have not survived. Othery underwent the same transformation at the same time, and here one of the surviving poppy-head benches bears the initials R.B. There is abundant evidence that many monastic houses did not neglect the fabric of parish churches that belonged to them but in fact did far more than their minimum responsibilities would have suggested.

Two miles beyond Chedzoy one comes to the outskirts of the town of Bridgwater, on the tidal river Parrett, a town whose medieval and later topography would make a good exercise in detailed reconstruction. The very name presents a problem, for it is called *Brugie* in Domesday Book, meaning 'bridge'. If there was a bridge over the Parrett at this point in the eleventh century, how could river-traffic have got as far upstream as Langport, Stathe, and lesser landing-places? The bridge would have been a timber structure at that date (stone bridges were unknown in England before the late twelfth century) and was probably high enough for boats to pass under it. In all probability, Bridgwater developed as a point of transhipment, at which sea-going vessels transferred their cargoes to boats or lighters, which then proceeded up-river into the heart of Somerset.

The town began to develop during the latter part of the twelfth century, a time of great expansion in English trade. In Domesday Book the picture is still one of an entirely rural and agricultural community, with a population of slaves (*servi*), villeins, bordars, and cottars, and of a lord's farm, villein farms, and smallholdings, with the usual meadow and pasture, and a water-mill. There is not the slightest hint of an urban community.

In the year 1200 William Brewer, lord of Bridgwater, obtained from King John a charter for the nascent town. It was henceforward to be a free borough, and to have a weekly market and an annual fair, and other burghal privileges including that of *lastage* which was the right to collect duty on freights and on vessels unloading there. Shortly after this (1202) Brewer obtained permission to build a castle for the protection of his little town and port, and about the same date he began building a new bridge over the Parrett. This was in all probability a stone bridge replacing the old timber structure.

Thus in the closing years of the twelfth century and the early years of the thirteenth, the town of Bridgwater acquired most of its major topographical features—market-place, castle, bridge, the quays, and perhaps its basic street-pattern. There is a reasonably good history of the town, by the standards of the time,[1] but the physical development of the town from the twelfth century onwards still awaits the worker who can interpret the visble scene as well as the written evidence.

[1] See A. H. Powell, *The Ancient Borough of Bridgwater* (1907), and *Bridgwater in the Later Days* (1908). The complete absence of any plan of the town is indicative, however, of the non-topographical approach to urban history.

Farewell to Fieldwork

I began this book by saying I had been born in Devon, in an ancient city surrounded by then unspoilt country which was full of interesting problems for an inquiring youngster. Now, towards the close of a working life but with the same inquiring mind, I live in the east midlands, not far from the edge of the wide enormous fens—it is about twenty miles to the Fen Edge near the Lincolnshire town of Bourne—and have the benefit of two distinctive stretches of country to study. The problems raised by these new landscapes are on the face of them very different from those I used to wrestle with forty years and more ago in the south-west, but certain basic questions remain the same. Once upon a time my vision stopped at the pages of Domesday Book and I was interested in tracing the continuity of rural life, in great detail, from the eleventh century to the present day. Now I look back increasingly to Roman times and beyond. I now believe that in many parts of England there has been an unbroken succession of life since the Iron Age, above all in the more fertile parts of the country but perhaps in less favoured regions also. The Teutonic School has done, in my view, great harm to early English history by postulating a catastrophic break between Roman Britain and Anglo-Saxon England. There are various common-sense reasons for rejecting this view. It was a pure assumption, but by adopting it the Teutonic School have bedevilled much history that has been written since.[1] Fortunately

[1] To develop this criticism would take half a book and would be quite out of place here. My O'Donnell lecture on 'Maps and Landscapes', already referred to, will develop this theme when it is published.

the tide of historical thinking seems to be turning against it.

The beauty of local history, and of the fieldwork connected with it, is that it involves so much close detail. It is micro-history. It uses the microscope upon a small piece of country and studies it without preconceptions, as far as this is humanly possible. A basic working knowledge of general English history is obviously desirable; but there is much to be said for being self-taught, for never having sat at the feet of some im-mense authority laying down the law in unforgettable terms. Instead, everything comes fresh, bright-polished, and newly-minted to the eager eye.

A few weeks ago Maxey was but a name on the map to me: now it is an obsession. The village lies in the deep Fens between Stamford and Spalding, just to the south of the little town of Market Deeping. Drifting across the Fens, too early for a luncheon at Spalding, I thought we would deviate to look at Maxey church, which I had never seen and about which I knew nothing, not having brought Pevsner's *Northamptonshire* with me.

We passed through a large and at first sight shapeless village, but no church appeared as we circled round the place and headed again for the open country. Then there it was, standing all alone far from the village, large and grey, massive Norman tower—locked. No matter: the seed had already been sown. Why was this great church standing alone, nearly a mile from the village? A church standing far from its parishioners is as provocative a start as the discovery of the body at the outset of a detective story.

When I returned home and gathered the few references around me and read in them, it grew even more mysterious and exciting. Normally, when an ancient parish church stands far from its village like this, one is safe in assuming that the village has migrated at some date towards another focus, per-haps a bridge or a busy main road. But it appeared that Saxo-Norman pottery had been found in the present village, indicat-ing that it had been settled at least by the eleventh century. Yet the church, which was built (rebuilt is more correct) between about 1100 and 1180, seemed to take no account of the new site of the village (if it was a new site). Moreover, a migration as early as the eleventh century is also something to be explained. This then was the basic problem which had been raised by the first sight of this grey Norman church standing so magnificently alone; but the more I read and thought about it the more complicated the topographical problems became.

Fortunately, there were sources for the early history and topography of Maxey beyond the average in usefulness, not least the remarkable recent excavation of a Dark Age settlement. There were also of course the customary maddening gaps in the sources.

The first step in any exploration of this kind is to ascertain the meaning of the place-name. Often it tells us nothing much, but in the case of Maxey it was a good start. It also raised further problems. The name first occurs in tenth-century charters as *Macuseige* with minor variations, with the meaning of 'Maccus's island'. Maccus is a personal name of Scandinavian origin, and in this instance represents the name of a Scandinavian overlord substituted for an earlier English name. The archaeological evidence, which will be considered in a moment, shows that there was a settlement here long before the Danish partition of this part of England in the late 870s.

'Maccus's island' lay between two arms of the Welland, one of which—that on the southern side—has been nearly eradicated on the one-inch map but is still a major obstacle on the ground. Even now this piece of country is virtually an island, about 4¾ miles long from east to west, and 1¾ miles across from north to south at its widest. A Roman road runs across the western end of the island, and a Roman canal (Car Dyke) cuts across the eastern side.

The island is now divided between the old ecclesiastical parishes of Maxey and Northborough, with a total area of 3379 acres between them.[1] This must have been the approximate area of Maccus's estate when he took over, perhaps towards the end of the ninth century.

The whole island is composed of Fen Margin Gravels, and

---

[1] The one-inch map shows a civil parish of Deeping Gate on the island also but this was taken out of Maxey at a late date and has no historical meaning.

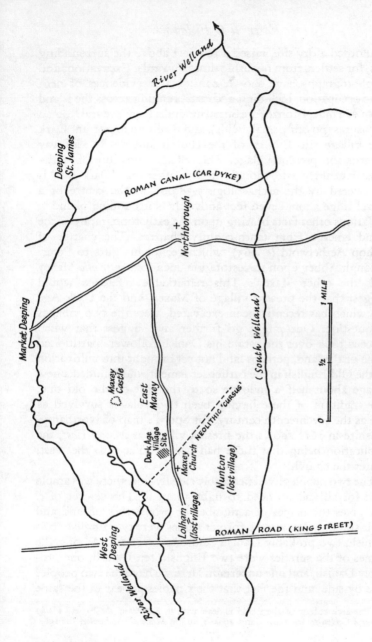

MAP VIII Maxey: The Island of Maccus. No attempt has been made to show all the archaeological and topographical features of this remarkable site, but only those which illustrate the text.

so afforded a dry site, raised a few feet above the surrounding fens, for settlers from neolithic times onwards. Excavations and air-photographs have shown considerable evidences of neo-lithic occupation, including a 'cursus' running across the island for over a mile; Bronze Age burial mounds; Iron Age and Roman enclosures (possibly small fields); and finally an important Dark Age village site E.N.E. of the church and nearly half-way towards the present village. This village—possibly of sixth-seventh century date, though no date other than 'Dark Age' is yet offered by the archaeologists—stood in the centre of a gravel ridge about seven feet above the surrounding plain.[1]

Various other facts bearing upon the early topography of the island emerge from tenth-century charters. The charter of Bishop Aethelwold (*c.* 963), which recites his gifts to Peter-borough Abbey upon its restoration, mentions *inter alia* Maxey and 'the other Maxey'. This remarkable reference would suggest that the present village of Maxey, and the Dark Age site which has recently been excavated, were the two villages in question. One might go further and suggest that when Maccus took over the estate his Danish followers partitioned some of the land, perhaps land not yet brought into cultivation by the Old English in the earlier settlement, and founded a new village about half a mile or so to the east of the old one. The tradition of there having been two villages survived as late as the seventeenth century, for Speed's map of Northamp-tonshire in 1611 shows the present village as *Maxey East*, the implication being that there had been a village to the west, nearer the church.

The two peoples lived peaceably side by side: there was ample land for all and no need to fight about it. The charter of *c.* 963 gives the names of a number of proprietors of land and their sureties. Among the former names were two English, two Danish, two probably Danish, and one uncertain. Among the names of the sureties were two English, ten Danish, one pro-bably Danish, and one uncertain. Here we have the two peoples side by side, and the fact that their names appear in the same

---

[1] The archaeology of the island is dealt with in *Reports of the Welland Valley Research Committee* for 1962–3 and 1963–4, and in *Medieval Archaeology* for 1964.

document would suggest that they were co-existing, to use the modern jargon, in a peaceful fashion.[1]

Unfortunately, Maxey is not separately recorded in Domesday Book. It then belonged to Peterborough Abbey and the abbey's lands are not distinguished from each other. Hence we cannot see whether the social structure of the two villages differed in some significant way in the eleventh century. When I wrote the history of the Leicestershire village of Wigston Magna some years ago, I was obliged to postulate from the evidence of Domesday Book that an English and a Scandinavian community existed side by side in 1086; and here too the Old English village had changed its name when the new Scandinavian overlord (*Vikingr*) took over the estate.

I cited several examples in Leicestershire of double vills of this kind, suggesting that the Danes either founded another village a short distance away from an Old English village or at least formed a distinct community in the original village, probably in a separate quarter. It seems likely that this is the explanation of the two villages at Maxey, the Old English village near the church and the Danish one to the east. The evidence of this mixture of peoples is still to be seen, for on entering the churchyard at Northborough, the other village on the old island, the first headstone that catches the eye is to some *Kettles*. This is a pure Danish personal name going back to the ninth and tenth centuries. And it may not be fanciful to see the other people of pre-Conquest days commemorated in another headstone a few yards away, to the *English* family. The fieldworker's day should always include the inspection of the churchyard.

Besides the two Maxeys, and Northborough already mentioned, there were at least two other early settlements on the island. These were Nunton and Lolham, one half a mile to the west of the church and the other about half a mile to the south. Nunton, now Nunton Lodge, was formerly a village. It was named after Nunna, certainly an Old English personal name, and first occurs in the charter of *c*. 963. Lolham, now Lolham Hall, was also a village. The derivation of the name is uncer-

[1] See 'A Dark Age Settlement at Maxey, Northants' in *Medieval Archaeology*, vol. VIII (1964), p. 22.

tain, but it stands beside King Street, a Roman road, between the two crossings of the Welland branches, a bleak cold spot for a good bit of the year. The most likely meaning of the name is a shelter of some kind (see *Place-Names of Northamptonshire*, p. 238). It is first recorded in a Thorney charter of *c.* 1150 but undoubtedly goes back as a settlement well into pre-Conquest times.

We now return to the problem of the parish church and its isolated position. One possible explanation is that with Nunton to the south, Lolham to the west, and the Maxeys to the east, the church was built at this lonely spot as being central to the four villages, or to the three villages if we assume that the first church was built before the Danish Conquest. This is a very plausible theory, but there are other possibilities which cannot be ruled out.

The simplest alternative explanation is that the Dark Age village extended much nearer to the church than the excavations recently made had revealed. The excavation was an emergency dig before extensive gravel diggings destroyed the site for ever, and did not claim to be exhaustive. Air photographs show a pattern of enclosures, some of them small enough to be homestead sites, in fields immediately to the east and west of the church. The seven rectangular buildings already found probably represent only a part of the Dark Age village. The parish church may originally have stood very close to the Old English village, the village which for some reason and at some unknown date ceased to exist.

But even this is not the end of the story, for a second visit to the church revealed a significant clue which had not been spotted on the first occasion. This was that the church was in fact built upon a distinct rise in the ground, which I estimated to be about five feet above the surrounding ground. Small differences like this are of much greater significance in this type of country than they would be anywhere else. Moreover, when one walks round the outside of the church this slight elevation seems to take the form of a circular mound, and one suddenly realizes that Maxey church may have been built here precisely because it was already a great burial mound, a hallowed site in prehistoric and perhaps later times. Such a continuity of hallowed sites from pre-Christian times into the Christian period is not unknown elsewhere. In Dorset the parish church of Moreton is built upon a conspicuous burial mound. Fimber church in Yorkshire is built upon a Bronze Age barrow which was later used as a pagan Anglian burial-place; and Edlesborough in Buckinghamshire was built upon 'Eadwulf's barrow' from which it takes its name.

There is clearly a wide range of fieldwork to be done in the old island of Maxey, though most of the new evidence will come from archaeological excavation of many periods rather than above-ground fieldwork. Air photographs show a remarkable amount of suggestive markings in the ground for the whole of the prehistoric period and running into Romano-British times. Both Nunton and Lolham are the sites of deserted medieval villages which could be recognized on the surface. Nunton consists today of Nunton Lodge and two cottages, but in the tax assessments of 1301 and 1524 it could muster eleven taxpayers, probably representing as many households. And at Lolham, now a Hall and two cottages, there were twelve taxpayers in 1301.

At Northborough there is the site of the Anglian *burh* to be discovered. It was 'north *burh*' in relation to the *burh* which subsequently became Peterborough. At Maxey itself the rather formless street-plan calls for exploration: it looks suspiciously like the remains of a larger and more symmetrical plan. I have no doubt that as one explored the ground and the documents relating to this island whole new ranges of inquiry would open up which are at the moment unsuspected.

Thus the small tract of country that one passes with scarcely a glance on the main road from Stamford to Spalding, of which the only conspicuous feature is the lonely church of St. Peter and St. Paul, has now become, even in this tentative exploration which leaves so much unanswered, an ancient island with a clear-cut identity of its own, its fertile loam occupied by men in neolithic times, in the Bronze and Iron Ages, by Romans, by early English, and by Danes, perhaps a continuous occupation so far as farming goes for thousands of years, its surface marked by dark lines and spots, by mounds, amid the wide acres of rustling barley today.

*   *   *

And now I turn at the last to the austere and lovely north of England, where I first began my working life, a province which has never lost its appeal for me, so utterly different from the misty ancestral hills of the south-west. It is to a village set upon a Pennine hill that I turn, a few miles to the west of the smoking pit of Halifax—the village of Heptonstall.

In a rare moment of exuberance, Nikolaus Pevsner describes Heptonstall as 'a very handsome hill village of dark stone houses with all kinds of minor architectural surprises'. It is indeed, and more than this. It is an almost untouched specimen of a West Yorkshire village, a truly native place, such a place as one would go a long way to see were it in a foreign country. Moreover, it contains mysteries—the ruined medieval church in its overcrowded churchyard, with a noble Early Victorian church within a few yards of it; the feeling of prosperity down to well into the nineteenth century, as seen for example in the new parish church, the Mechanics Institution built in 1868, and the wool warehouses; and then the evidences of decay. What happened at Heptonstall to leave it fossilized on its steep hill, while the serried mills and terraced houses down below at Hebden Bridge multipled decade by decade?

Until a few years ago, Heptonstall retained its streets paved with stone setts; and even now it gives one the feeling that not much has changed since the early nineteenth century. Everything is built of stone, the two famous stones of these parts: Gaisby Rock from the quarries just south-east of Shipley near Bradford, and the Elland Flags, both notable building stones from the bottom of the Coal Measures, with a coarser Millstone Grit for poorer work here and there. And as Pevsner says, the stone has blackened everywhere, absorbing the mill-smoke drifting up from the deep Hebden valley, so giving an air of even greater age and dignity to the whole place.

Almost nothing seems to have been written about the history

of Heptonstall. It was part of the distant manor of Wakefield, which accounts for its not being mentioned separately in Domesday Book though it has an Old English name and undoubtedly existed before the Norman Conquest; and ecclesiastically it was one of the dozen or so chapelries of the vast parish of Halifax, usually regarded as the largest ancient parish in the whole of England. Heptonstall was the most westerly of the chapelries, bordering upon Lancashire where the moors rise to over 1,500 ft. at Black Hameldon. Much of the township lies over a thousand feet up, originally mostly rough grazing but now dotted with perhaps a score of hamlets, detached farmhouses and cottages surrounded by, for the most part, very small stone-walled fields, which make a highly characteristic pattern on the 2½-inch map. Thus the hamlets are not tightly-knit but loosely spread over perhaps two or three hundred yards or more.

What is the origin of Heptonstall? It is not recorded by name until the middle of the thirteenth century, but it was already centuries old by then. The plunging valley down below was the Hebden—'the wild-rose valley' from its most conspicuous plant—and this was Hebden *stall*, a word that is found often on these high lands and seems to have the original meaning of a cattle farm, a vaccary. The valleys in this part of the Pennines are steep-sided and were so thickly wooded that most settlement took place on the higher ground. The valley floor was not effectively occupied until the use of water-power for industrial machinery.

Heptonstall stands on the side of a hill, rising from 750 feet at one end to 900 feet at the other, so that its narrow main street itself is a hard climb all the way. As the old main road from Halifax to Burnley, it was one of the few ancient crossings of the Pennines (called The Long Causeway for some miles on the top), probably prehistoric in origin, and was the main reason for the siting of the upland village.

It is conceivable that for a long period Heptonstall was merely a summer settlement, like other *stalls* on these moors, to which men migrated from older places for the rough grazing for a few months of the year; but this is something that needs working out from the records of these *stalls*. Possibly by the twelfth century it was becoming, or had just become, a permanent settlement, but this is pure speculation. The first church is said to have been built about 1340, and to have been rebuilt in the closing years of the fifteenth century, though Pevsner dates the masonry of the lower part of the old tower as thirteenth century. The remainder of the old church, now ruined, is all of Perpendicular date. Some repair work was done upon it in the seventeenth century, which was a prosperous time for all the country around; but what happened to allow the old church to fall into such decay that it was decided to build an entirely new one in the early 1850s and to dismantle the old? It should not be difficult to find out.

As for the other buildings of the village, there is everything from the sixteenth century to the nineteenth. The Court House in the main street is said to be the oldest house in the place, but does not look it from the outside. Up a side street is White Hall, with the date 1578 on a massive lintel over the gateway. The attractive Grammar School was founded in 1642 and survives intact beside the churchyard. Not far away is the Mechanics Institution, built in 1868, with the motto over its doorway 'Man Know Thyself', so redolent of nineteenth-century self-education and optimism. The vernacular domestic building wants studying house by house. Not much seems to remain of the industrial period except a large wool warehouse or two, but much more could come to light in a close inspection of interiors. The countryside beyond the village is more obviously rewarding this respect.

The early directories of the West Riding are a particularly useful source for the social and economic, and hence the building, history of places like Heptonstall, only qualified in this instance by the fact that the boundaries of the township reached to the valley bottom and included part of Hebden Bridge. So we do not know precisely where the five cotton manufacturers and the two cotton spinners had their premises, as recorded in Baines's directory for 1822; whether up on the top (which seems unlikely) or down the bottom near the water-power. The 1847 directory shows further changes, much more growth down at Hebden Bridge, and later directories would complete the story until the first edition of the 25-inch map in the 1880's gives us something very precise to go upon. Hebden Bridge got its own church in 1833. Yorkshire was one of the counties surveyed on the six-inch scale in the years 1840–54, and these maps too should be consulted.

It is already clear from what has been said about Hebden Bridge that Heptonstall cannot be studied in isolation. As a village it depended upon a huge area around. The industrial history of the early nineteenth century, and perhaps even the the eighteenth, of Heptonstall and Hebden Bridge cannot be considered apart; and when we examine the landscape to the west of Heptonstall, up on the high ground, we see abundant evidence of an earlier industrial system—the so-called Domestic System—in the lonely hamlets and farms that makes it imperative to consider the township and its history as a whole and not merely the village we began with.

In his tour through England and Wales (*c.* 1727) Defoe has a famous description of the country around Halifax, which included of course Heptonstall and its hamlets. As he came nearer to Halifax 'we found the houses thicker, and the villages greater in every bottom; and not only so, but the sides of the hills, which were very steep every way, were spread with houses, and that very thick; for the land being divided into small enclosures, that is to say, from two acres to six or seven acres each, seldom more; every three or four pieces of land had a house belonging to it. . . . We found the country, in short, one continued village . . . hardly a house standing out of a speaking distance from another . . . and we could see that almost at every house there was a tenter, and almost on every tenter a piece of cloth, or kersie, or shalloon, for they are the three articles of that country's labour.'

The master-clothier was often if not usually a yeoman-farmer. He bought the wool at Halifax or some other great market, brought it back by pack-horse to his isolated hamlet and put it out to the weavers in their cottages, who wove it into the cloths that Defoe saw drying in the sun, and then collected it for delivery in the nearest market-town. So we generally find that the typical set-up is like that to be seen at Greenwood Lee a few miles west of Heptonstall on the road over the moors to Colne. Here there is a good early seventeenth-century clothier's house, almost a small manor-house type, with ample room for storage and stabling for pack-horses; and scattered along the road are a number of detached cottages, really small farmhouses, of seventeenth-century date which were the homes of the farmer-weavers, the 'manufacturers' of Defoe's day. It was these small men who did the weaving in their own houses, on an upper floor that gives itself away immediately by the long window, running almost its full length. Some of these windows, designed to throw the maximum light on the loom at work, may have six, eight, or ten lights. Two old inns at Slaithwaite, near Huddersfield, have each an upper window of fourteen lights, and at Marsden there is a rear window of nineteen lights, though this perhaps represents the next stage in industrial organization—a workshop for several people rather than a true cottage-industry.

The moors around Halifax are particularly rich in these buildings of the great days of the woollen industry under the Domestic System, and to a lesser extent the country around Huddersfield. The latter has been described in Crump and Ghorbal, *History of the Huddersfield Woollen Industry* (Huddersfield, 1935), especially pages 43 to 59. The West Yorkshire woollen trade developed remarkably quickly after 1688. When Defoe was writing it had had some forty years of continued prosperity, due mainly to the prodigious demand for clothing the army in the almost incessant wars of that period; and we see the visual evidence of this in the thousands of buildings of the late seventeenth and early eighteenth century all over this wonderful countryside.

But we are still left with the problem of why Heptonstall went into decay. I suppose the general reason was that the water-power was down in the valley bottom, when the real Industrial Revolution began. The early mills went up in Hebden Bridge and then came the Rochdale Canal, in 1804, the first canal to cross the Pennines. On the Yorkshire side it ran along the valley-bottom to Sowerby Bridge, where it joined

the Calder and Hebble Navigation. So with everything happening a mile away and far below, Heptonstall decayed slowly on
its hill-top. But its history, and that of its dependent Hebden
Bridge, remains to be written. I suspect that Hebden Bridge
itself has a modest industrial beginning in the sixteenth century,
perhaps with fulling-mills. The detailed industrial archaeology
of this fascinating piece of country from the moorland clothiers'
houses of Jacobean days to the great Victorian mills, the nineteenth-century industrial housing, and the canal too, calls out
for the field-worker's attention before things change too much
beyond recall.

★   ★   ★

There is no opposition between fieldwork and documents.
Both are essential to the good local historian. Behind a good deal
of work in the field and in the street are documents that help to
throw more light on what is being studied; and behind a
good many documents lies much valuable fieldwork if only the
unimaginative 'researcher' had the wit to see it. Most acade-
mically-trained historians are completely blind to the existence
and value of visual evidence. Visually speaking, they are still
illiterate.

That great French historian, Marc Bloch, believed that historians should make more use of all kinds of evidence besides
that of documents. We must use all the material evidence of the
past, and go beyond even that at times to study the evidence of
vegetation. I quote again what Sir George Stapledon said, that
'vegetation accurately read is a remorseless and wholly objective
historian'; and again would go farther and observe that the
same could be said of buildings however humble and unpreten-
tious. That is why I attach so much importance in this book
to the study of buildings at all social levels. Indeed everything
in our present landscape tells us something about the past if
only we can learn how to interpret it. Bloch was aware of this
too. In his posthumous book, *The Historian's Craft,* which I
commend to all good local historians who seek to rise above a
lowly antiquarian level, there are many wise remarks; and there
is one in particular that I wish to end on: 'Behind the features

of the landscape, behind tools or machinery, behind what appears to be the most formalized written documents, and behind institutions, which seem almost entirely detached from their founders, there are men, and it is men that history seeks to grasp. Failing that, it will be at best but an exercise in erudition. The good historian is like the giant of the fairy tale. He knows that wherever he catches the scent of human flesh, there his quarry lies.'

In this book it might appear at first sight that I have been very little concerned with men. It is primarily a book about the problems and methods of fieldwork, about techniques and sources; but behind the evidence, whatever form it may take, one must strive to hear the men and women of the past talking and working, and creating what has come down to us, after so long a time, for our present enjoyment.

Index

Ablington (Gloucs.), 78
Adult education, classes, 12
Alfred the Great, 15
All Saints Church, Stamford (Lincs.), 25
All Souls College, Oxford, 74
Allcroft, Hadrian, *Earthwork of England*, 30, 55
Alnwick (Conzen), 66, 72
Alresford, New (Hants.), 92
Alresford, Old (Hants.), 92
Alvechurch (Worcs.), 88
Ancient Borough of Bridgwater (Powell), 169 n.
'Ancient Highways of Dorset, Somerset, and South-West England' (Grundy). *Arch. Journal, Vols XCIV, and XCV, 1934, 1935*, 136 n.
Ancient Trackways of Wessex (Timperley *and* Brill), 137
Anglo-Saxon land charters, 34–40
Anglo-Saxon landscapes, 34–47
Appleby Magna (Leics.), 55
Archaeologia Cantiana, Vol. LXXVII (1962), 'Some early Kentish Estate maps and their portrayal of field boundaries' (Baker), 76 n.
Archaeological Journal, Vol. CX, 1964, 'Origins and early growth of Northampton' (Lee), 66
Archaeology in the Field (Crawford), 50, 53, 136, 137 n.
Aspects of Archaeology in Britain and Beyond, 'The Jurassic Way' (Grimes), 137
Axe, River (Som.), 60, 61
Axbridge (Som.), 60

Baker, Alan, *Archaeologia Cantiana*, 'Some Fields and Farms of Medieval Kent', 76

Baker, Alan, 'Field-patterns in Seventeenth-century Kent', *Geography, Vol. 59 (1965)*, 76 n.
Baker, Alan, 'Some early Kentish Estate maps and a note on their portrayal of field boundaries', *Arch. Cant., Vol. LXXVII, 1962, pgs. 177–84*, 76 n.
Bargain and Sale, deeds of, 115
Barley, Maurice, *The English Farmhouse and Cottage*, 22 n.
Barnsley (Yorks.), 92
Barton-upon-Irwell (Lancs.), 87
Bartonbury, Down St. Mary (Devon), 107–11
Beach-lines, 27, 33
Beccles (Suffolk), 60
Bedfordshire, 54, 95
Bedwyn (Wilts.), Saxon charter, 36
Beeby (Leics.), 82
Beresford, Maurice, *History on the ground*, 59
Beresford, Maurice, *Lost Villages of England*, 58
Beresford, Maurice *and* St. Joseph, J. K., *Medieval England: An Aerial Survey*, 59, 91
Berkshire, 59 n., 89
Berkshire Archaeological Journal, 'Introduction to a First List of Deserted Medieval Village Sites in Berkshire', 59 n.
Berkshire, deserted villages, 59 n.
Bibury (Gloucs.), 78–9
Binneford, Stockleigh English (Devon), 112
Birch, *Cartularium Saxonicum* (London, 1885–93), 37
'Bitterne after the Romans' (Crawford), 158 n.

Index

Blacklands, meaning of, 92–3
Blakeney (Norfolk), 63, 156–7
Bleadon (Som.), 61
Bloch, Marc, *The Historian's Craft*, 183
Borough and Town: a Study of Urban Origins in England (Stephenson), 164
Boundaries, 18, 19, 34–40, 44, 53, 66, 72, 76 n., 119 n., 123, 124, 132, 148, 159 (*see also* Hedge-banks, Walls)
Bowley (Devon), 44
Brackley (Northants.), 91
Brancaster (Norfolk), 63
Bratton Fleming (Devon), 99, 126, 127, 129
Brettenham (Norfolk), 86
Bridgwater (Som.), 60, 61, 168–9
Bridgwater in the Later Days (Powell), 169 n.
Bristol, 90
Brittany, trade with, 61
Brokenborough (Wilts.), Saxon charter, 36
Buckenham, New (Norfolk), 90–1
Buckenham, Old (Norfolk), 90
Buckfast Abbey (Devon), 109, 110
Buckinghamshire, 89
Buckworth (Hunts.), 119, 120–1
Bullock Road (Hunts.), 144, 145
Burbage (Wilts.), Saxon charter, 36
Bure, River (Norfolk), 60
Burgess, L. A., *The Origins of Southampton*, 66
Burnham (Norfolk), 63
Burwell (Cambs.), 62

Cadbury (Devon), 15–21, 41, 44–5, 128
Cadeleigh (Devon), 44
Caister (Norfolk), 79–80
Calthorpe's Bank (Norfolk), 151
Cam, River, 62
Cambridgeshire, 62, 65
Cantor, L. M., 'The Medieval Parks of South Staffordshire', *Transactions of the Birmingham Archaeological Society*, 51 n.
Cantor, L. M. *and* Wilson, J. D., 'The Medieval Deer-Parks of Dorset', *Proceedings of the Dorset Natural History and Archaeological Society*, 51 n.
Cattle roads, 143–7, 165
Centuriation, Roman, 139–40
Chambers, J. D., *A Century of Nottingham History*, 72
Chambers, J. D., *Modern Nottingham in the making*, 72
Chancery Miscellanea, 53

'Changes in Farm and Field Boundaries in the Nineteenth Century' (Coppock), 119 n.
Chapeltown, Higher and Lower (Devon), 16
Chapman, S. D., 'Working class housing in Nottingham during the Industrial Revolution', *Transactions of the Thoroton Society, 1963*, 67 n.
Chard (Som.), 91–2
Cheddar Water (Som.), 60
Chedzoy (Som.), 165, 168
Chelfham (Devon), 126–7
Cheriton Bishop (Devon), 124
Cheriton, meaning of, 89
Cheshire, 89
'Chessels', meaning of, 93
Chilton (Devon), 15
Chirton (Wilts.), 89
Chitty, L. F., 'The Clun-Clee Ridgeway . . .', *Culture and Environment: Essays in Honour of Sir Cyril Fox*, 137
Choseley (Norfolk), 59, 93
Chumhill (Devon), 126–7, 128
Church Farm, Cadbury (Devon), 16, 18, 45
Churton (Cheshire), 89
Claybrook (Leics.), 101–3
Cley (Norfolk), 63, 150–1, 154, 156
'The Clun-Clee Ridgeway' (Chitty), 137
Coastline of England and Wales (Steer), 151 n.
Cokes of Holkham, 74
Colyton (Devon), 97
Combwich (Som.), 61
Common Lands of England and Wales (Hoskins *and* Stamp), 146 n.
Compton Episcopi (Som.), 61
Continuity in English history, 19, 79, 79 n., 170–1 and *passim*
Conzen, M. R. G., *Alnwick*, 66, 72
Coppock, J. T., 'Changes in Farm and Field Boundaries in the Nineteenth Century', 119 n.
Cornwall, 37, 42, 100–1, 113
Courtenays, earls of Devon, 105
Cox, J. C., *How to write the History of a parish*, 54
Cox, J. C., *Royal Forests of England*, 54
Cozens-Hardy, B., 151 n.
Crawford, O. G. S., *Archaeology in the Field*, 50, 52, 53, 136, 137 n.
Crawford, O. G. S., 'Bitterne after the Romans', 158 n.
Cromer (Norfolk), 63, 79

Index

Crow Close (Notts.), 55

'Dark Age Settlement at Maxey, Northants', *Medieval Archaeology, Vol. VIII, 1964,* 175 n.
Dartmoor (Devon), 21, 23, 31, 147
Dartmouth (Devon), 61
Deer-parks, 51–4
Demesne farms, 41–5, 48, 87
Derbyshire, 12
Dersingham (Norfolk), 63
Deserted villages, 29–31, 50, 55–9
Devon, 15–21, 23, 28, 31, 37, 40–2, 44–5, 46, 52–3, 61, 68–70, 72, 74, 76–7, 88, 90, 91, 92, 93, 97–9, 104–5, 107–11, 112, 113, 114 n., 115, 122, 123, 123 n., 124, 126–9, 138, 147
Devon and Exeter Institution (Exeter), 105
Devon Monastic Lands, 1536–58 (Youings), 110 n.
Dictionary of English Place-names (Ekwall), 77
Dining-room, degradation of, 23
Domesday Book, 16–18, 25, 34, 40–7, 52, 56, 73, 83, 84, 89, 90, 92, 110, 116, 127, 129, 133, 155, 157, 158, 161, 166, 167, 168, 175
Domesday Book and Beyond (Maitland), 17, 117
Dorset, 51 n., 52
Dorset, Medieval deer-parks, 51 n.
Double vills, 174–5
Down St. Mary (Devon), 107–11
Downend (Som.), 61
Drove Roads, 144, 145
Drove Roads of Scotland (Haldane), 144 n.
Duckham, B. F., 'Inland Waterways: some sources for their History', 64
Duckham, B. F., *Navigable Rivers of Yorkshire,* 60 n.
Dunwich (Suffolk), 49
Durham, Co., 49, 119
Duryard (Devon), 52
Dyos, H. J., *Victorian Suburb,* 71

'Early Bounds of Wanborough and Little Hinton' (Thomson), 39–40
Early Charters of Devon and Cornwall (Finberg), 37
Early Charters of Eastern England (Hart), 36, 37
Early Charters of Essex (Hart), 37
Early Charters of the West Midlands (Finberg), 37, 39

Early Charters of Wessex (Finberg), 37, 160 n.
Earthwork of England (Allcroft), 30, 55
East Anglia, 32, 36, 37, 40–1 (*see also* Norfolk, Suffolk)
East Down (Devon), 114 n.
Eccles (Kent), 86
Eccles (Norfolk), 84–5, 86
Eccleshall (Staffs.), 87
Eccleshill (Lancs.), 87
Ecclesiastical Parish Boundaries, 39
Eccleston (Lancs.), 87
Ekwall, *Dictionary of English Place-names,* 77
Ely (Cambs.), 65
Emery, F. V., 'Moated settlements in England', 54, 55
Emmison, F. G., *Jacobean Household Inventories,* 95
Enclosure Awards and Maps, 122
Enclosure, parliamentary, 74–5, 122, 132
Endacott, Higher and Lower (Devon), 16
English Deer Parks (Shirley), 53, 54
English Farmhouse and Cottage (Barley), 22 n.
English Field Systems (Gray), 135
English Place-name Society, 77, 78
Enrolled Deeds, 115
Essex, 37, 54, 95
Exeter (Devon), 52, 68–70, 104–5, 138
Exeter Houses (Portman), 105 n.
Exning (Suffolk), 90
Exploration of Towns, 24–9

Farm and Cottage Inventories of Mid-Essex (Steer), 95
Farm boundaries, 18–19
Farm history, sources, 111–16
Farmsteads, 19–24, 41–5, 52, 56, 75, 107–16
Fen Ditton (Cambs.), 62
Field Archaeology (H.M.S.O.), 55, 59, 93, 139, 155
Field boundaries, 123, 132
'Field patterns in seventeenth-century Kent' (Baker), 76 n.
Field-systems, 135 (*see also* Field Walls)
Field walls, 130–5
Finberg, H. P. R., *Early Charters of Devon and Cornwall,* 37
Finberg, H. P. R., *Early Charters of Wessex,* 37, 160 n.

Finberg, H. P. R., *Early Charters of the West Midlands*, 37, 39
Finberg, H. P. R., 'Recent Progress in English Agrarian History', 135
Finberg, H. P. R., 'Roman and Saxon Withington', 79 n.
Finberg, H. P. R., on Shropshire charters, 36
Finberg, H. P. R., *Tavistock Abbey*, 123 n.
Flegg (Norfolk), 80–2
Flora of hedges, 124–30
Food, good, neglect of in England, 23
Fordwich (Kent), 60
Forests, 51–4
Foure Bookes of Husbandry (Googe), 130

Geografiska Annaler, 'Recent Progress in English Agrarian History' (Finberg), 135
Geography, 'Field patterns in seventeenth-century Kent' (Baker), 76 n.,
Geography, 'Moated settlements in England' (Emery), 54, 55
Glandford (Norfolk), 150, 151, 153, 154
Glaven, River (Norfolk), 150–1
Glebe terriers, 97–104
Gloucester, 49
Gloucestershire, 49, 78–9, 79 n., 88, 92
Godwin, H., 'Prehistoric wooden trackways of the Somerset levels . . . ' 165 n.
Googe, Barnaby, *Foure Bookes of Husbandry*, 130
Gough, J. W., *Mines of Mendip*, 61
Gramborough Hill (Norfolk), 155, 156
Gray, H. L., *English Field Systems*, 135
Great Casterton (Rutland), 25
Great North Road, 24–5
Great Ouse, River, 62
Great Rebuilding (1570–1640), 22–3
Great Yarmouth (Norfolk), 26–8, 33, 65, 91, 154
Green, B. *and* Young, R., *Norwich: the growth of a city*, 66
Green, Charles, 12, 83 n.
Green Bank (Norfolk), 140, 142
Grimes, W. F., 'The Jurassic Way', 137
Grundy, G. B., 'The Ancient Highways of Dorset, Somerset, and South-West England', 136 n.
Grundy, G. B., 'Saxon charters and field-names in Gloucestershire', 78
Grundy, G. B., 'The Saxon charters and Field Names of Somerset', 37, 160 n.

Haldane, A. R. B., *The Drove Roads of Scotland*, 144 n.
Halse (Northants.), 91
Halstow, Dunsford (Devon), 112
Hamilton (Leics.), 93
Hampshire, 66, 89, 92, 158 n.
Handbook for Travellers in Surrey (Murray), 92
Happisburgh (Norfolk), 85
Hardington (Som.), 100
Harlington (Beds.), 54
Hart, C. R., *Early Charters of Eastern England*, 36, 37
Hart, C. R., *Early Charters of Essex*, 37
Heacham (Norfolk), 63
Hearth Tax Assessments, 57, 114–15
Hebden Bridge (Yorks.), 180–1
Hedge-bank flora, 124–30
Hedge-banks, 18, 117, 118–35
Hedge-maps, 119, 129
Hedges, dating of, 33, 134–5
Hedges and walls, 117–35
Hedon (Yorks.), 27
Hemsby (Norfolk), 80
Heptonstall (Yorks.), 178–83
Herefordshire, 18, 88
Hertford (Herts.), 29
Hertfordshire, 28–9
Hickling (Norfolk), 84
Historians, blindness to visual evidence, 32, 183–4
Historians Guide to Ordnance Survey Maps, 70–1
History on the ground (Beresford), 59
Holkham (Norfolk), 74
Holme-next-the-Sea (Norfolk), 140–1
Holt (Norfolk), 157
Honeychurch (Devon), 88
Honiton (Devon), 91
Hooperhayne, Colyton (Devon), 97
Horn Park (Dorset), 52
Horsey (Norfolk), 83–4
Hoskins, W. G., *The Heritage of Leicestershire*, 55 n.
Hoskins, W. G., *Leicestershire: The History of the Landscape*, 75 n.
Hoskins, W. G., *Local History in England*, 11, 65, 95 n., 106
Hoskins, W. G., *Making of the English Landscape*, 32, 75 n., 92, 148 n.
Hoskins, W. G., *Midland Peasant*, 71, 104, 116
Hoskins, W. G., *Provincial England*, 17, 18 n., 23 n., 41, 42, 59, 128, 148 n., 160 n.

Hoskins, W. G. *and* Stamp, L. D., *The Common Lands of England and Wales*, 146 n.
Hound Tor, Dartmoor (Devon), 31
Housekeeping money, car run on, 23
Houses, 67–71, 94–106
Huddersfield Woollen Industry (Crump and Ghorbal), 182
Hughes, P. G., *Wales and the Drovers*, 144 n.
Hundred Rolls, 56, 110
Hunstanton (Norfolk), 63
Hunt, Philip, *Notes on Medieval Melton Mowbray*, 138 n.
Huntingdonshire, 55, 119, 144–5
Hurst, J. G., 59
Hythe (Som.), 60, 61

Ilchester (Som.), 60
Ilketshall (Suffolk), 143
Industrial Archaeology, 11–12
'Inland Waterways: Some sources for their History' (Duckham), 64
Inquisitions post mortem, 49–50
Inventories, kinds of, 95–7
Ipswich (Suffolk), 23, 66
Ismere (Worcs.), 34–5

Jacobean Household Inventories (Emmison), 95
Journal of Industrial Archaeology, 11
'Jurassic Way' (Grimes), 137

Kelling (Norfolk), 157–9
Kemble, *Codex Diplomaticus Aevi Saxonici* (London, 1839–48), 37
Kennedy, P. A., *Nottinghamshire Household Inventories*, 95
Kent, 48–9, 60, 74, 76, 76 n., 86 n., 91, 95, 96, 113, 136, 139
Kentisbury (Devon), 42
Kersey (Suffolk), 49
King's Lynn (Norfolk), 23, 63, 65
Kirby's Inquest, 1285, 134
Knaptoft (Leics.), 30, 43, 55, 56, 57, 59

Lancashire, 87
Land Charters (Saxon), 34–40
Land Tax Assessments, 114
Landing-places, lists of, 62–3
Landscapes, 29–33, 34–47
Lanes, 136–49
Langport (Som.), 60, 90, 160–5
Law of Property Act, 1925, 111
Lee, Frank, 'Origins and early growth of Northampton', 66

Leicester, 67, 70
Leicester Domestic Mission, 70
Leicestershire, 30, 31, 40, 43, 46, 49, 54, 55–9, 67, 70, 71, 74, 75, 75 n., 79, 80, 82, 88, 93, 96, 101–3, 104, 113, 115, 137–8, 138 n., 175
Leicestershire: the History of the Landscape (Hoskins), 75 n.
'Lellesheie' (Suffolk), 49
Leominster (Herefordshire), 88
Lessingham (Norfolk), 84
Lincolnshire, 24–6, 82, 92, 138, 156 n.
Lincolnshire Architectural and Archaeological Society Reports and Papers, 156 n.
Linton, Wharfedale (Yorks.), 131 (map), 132, 133, 134
Local History in England (Hoskins), 11, 65, 95 n., 106
Lord and the Landscape (Thorpe), 76 n.
Lost villages of England (Beresford), 58

Maitland, F. W., *Domesday Book and Beyond*, 17, 117
Malthouses, 28
Manorial boundaries, 44
Manorial records, 115
Manors, 48–50
Maps, 16–17, 28–9, 38–9, 52, 58, 63–4, 70–1, 74–6, 76 n., 113–14, 119–24, 139, 140, 141, 162–3, 173
Margary, I. D., *Roman Roads in Britain*, 139
Margary, I. D., *Roman Ways in the Weald*, 136, 139
Market Bosworth (Leics.), 88
Market-places, 25, 29, 66, 169
Marshwood (Dorset), 52
Maxey (Northants.), 171–7
Medieval Archaeology, 31
'Medieval Deer-Parks of Dorset' (Cantor *and* Wilson), 51 n.
Medieval England: an aerial Survey (Beresford *and* St. Joseph), 59, 91
Melling, E. *and* Oakley, A., *Some Kentish Houses*, 95, 96
Melton Mowbray (Leics.), 88, 137–8
Mendip, Mines of (Gough), 61
Midland Peasant (Hoskins), 71, 104, 116
Mines of Mendip (Gough), 61
Minster, significance of, 88
Miscellaneous Inquisitions, 48, 149, 152
Moated homesteads, 54–5
'Moated Settlements in England (Emery), 54–5
Moated sites, 58

Mockham Down (Devon), 126
Modern Nottingham in the Making (Chambers), 72
Monastic Giants, Particulars for, 110 n.
Mother-churches, 88–9

Navigable Rivers of Yorkshire (Duckham), 60 n.
New Forest (Hants.), 89
Newark (Notts.), 89
Newbald (Yorks.), 89
Newbury (Berks.), 89
Newcomen Society, *Transactions*, 12
Newland, meaning of, 90
Newmarket (Suffolk), 90
Newport, meaning of, 89
Newport Pagnell (Bucks.), 89
Newspapers, local, value of, 70
Newtimber (Sussex), 89
Newton, significance of, 89
Norfolk, 23, 26–8, 32, 33, 40, 58, 59, 60, 63, 64, 65, 66, 74, 79–85, 86, 90–1, 93, 119, 140–2, 142 n., 150–9
Norfolk Archaeology, 158
North Country Wills and Inventories (Surtees Society), 95
Northampton, 25
Northamptonshire, deserted villages, 31, 31 n., 58 n., 171
Northants., 25, 31, 31 n., 58 n., 66, 90, 91, 113, 171–8
Northborough (Northants.), 177–8
Northumberland, 66, 72
Norwich, 60
Norwich: the growth of a city (Green and Young), 66
Nottingham, 25
Nottinghamshire, 25, 30, 55, 67 n., 72, 89, 90, 95
Nottinghamshire Household Inventories (Kennedy), 95

Offa's Dyke, 52
Offchurch (Warwicks.), 88
Old (Northants.), 90
Old Hays (Leics.), 54
Old North Road, 25
Old Straight Track (Watkins), 137
Old Town, significance of, 91
Old Woking (Surrey), 92
Oldbarrow (Warwicks.), 90
Oldcoates (Notts.), 90
Oldland (Gloucs.), 92
'Origins and early growth of Northampton' (Lee), 66
Origins of Southampton (Burgess), 66

Ormesby (Norfolk), 80
Othery (Som.), 166
Outwell (Cambs.), 62
Oxford, 138
Oxfordshire, 31 n., 50, 57, 58 n., 74, 82, 86–7, 92, 138
Oxfordshire, deserted villages, 31 n., 58 n.

Pagan worship, 19
Palling (Norfolk), 84
Pannell, J. P. M., *Techniques of Industrial Archaeology*, 12 n.
Parish boundaries, 39, 66
Parks and forests, 51–4
Parliamentary enclosure movement, 74–5, 132
Parrett, River (Som.), 60, 61, 129, 160, 161, 168
Particulars for Grants, Monastic, 110 n.
Peddars Way (Roman road), 140, 142
Pennine Walls (Raistrick), 130, 131
Pevsner, N., *Northamptonshire*, 171
Place-names, 77–93
Place-names, Danish, 80
Place-names, Lancashire, 87
Place-names, Norfolk, 79–85
Place-names and ancient Churches, 85–8
Place-names of Northamptonshire, 176
Portland (Stamford), 25
Portman, Derek, *Exeter Houses*, 105 n.
Posbury (Devon), 111
Potters Marston (Leics.), 55
Powell, A. H., *Bridgwater in the Later Days*, 169 n.
Powell, A. H., *The Ancient Borough of Bridgwater*, 169 n.
'Prehistoric wooden trackways of the Somerset levels . . .' (Godwin), 165 n.
Prince, H. C., 'The Tithe Surveys of the Mid-Nineteenth Century', 113 n.
Probate inventories, 95–7, 105
Property boundaries, importance of, 72
Provincial England (Hoskins), 17, 18 n., 23 n., 41, 42, 59, 128, 148 n., 160 n.
Pucklechurch (Gloucs.), 88

Rackley (Som.), 60, 61
Raddon Hills (Devon), 44, 128
Raistrick, Arthur, *Pennine Walls*, 130, 131
Rebuilding, Great (1570–1640), 22, 23 n.
Reports of the Welland Valley Research Committee, 174 n.

River Navigation in England (Willan), 60 n.
River ports, 59–64
Roads, 136–49 and *passim*
Roads, cattle, 143–7, 165
Roads, Roman, 138–43
'Roman and Saxon Withington' (Finberg), 79 n.
'Roman Colony near Brancaster' (Ward), 142 n.
Roman roads, 138–43
Roman Roads in Britain (Margary), 139
Roman ways in the Weald (Margary), 136, 139
Romano-British temple, Cadbury (Devon), 16, 19
Romney, New (Kent), 91
Romney, Old (Kent), 91
Rows, Great Yarmouth, 26–7
Royal Forests of England (Cox), 54
Russell, P., *A History of Torquay*, 72
Rutland, 25, 31

St. Mary's Church, Stamford (Lincs.), 24–5
St. Michael's Church, Cadbury (Devon), 19
St. Peter's Church, Stamford (Lincs.), 25
Salford (Lancs.), 87
Salisbury, 91
Salop (Shropshire), 36, 49, 60, 113, 122, 137, 147
Salthouse (Norfolk), 63, 64, 154, 155, 156, 158
Sarum, New (Wilts.), 91
Saxby (Leics.), 82
Saxon charters, 34–40, 116, 117
'Saxon charters and field-names in Gloucestershire' (Grundy), 78
'The Saxon charters and field-names of Somerset' (Grundy), 37, 160 n.
'The Saxon Land Charters of Wiltshire' (Thomson), 36
Schoston (Co. Durham), 49
Scratby (Norfolk), 80
Severn, River, 60
Shardlow (Derbyshire), 11
Shirley, Evelyn, *English Deer Parks*, 53, 54
Shrewsbury (Salop), 60
Sileby (Leics.), 75
Silverton (Devon), 46
Snettisham (Norfolk), 63
Some Kentish Houses (Melling and Oakley), 95, 96

Somercotes (Lincs.), 82, 92
Somerset, 37, 60, 61, 90, 91–2, 100, 115, 129, 159–69, 169 n.
Somerton (Norfolk), 82–3
Somerton (Oxon.), 82, 92
Somerton (Som.), 159–60
South Elmham (Suffolk), 142–3
South Wigston (Leics.), 71
Special Commissions (Chancery), 53
Special Commissions (Exchequer), 97
Staffordshire, 51 n., 87
Staffordshire, Medieval deer-parks, 51 n.
Stamford (Lincs.), 24–6, 138
Stathe (Som.), 61
Steeple Barton (Oxon.), 50
Steer, Francis, *Farm and Cottage Inventories of Mid-Essex*, 95
Steer, J. A., *Coastline of England and Wales*, 151 n.
Stephenson, Carl, *Borough and Town: a Study of Urban Origins in England*, 164
Stockleigh Pomeroy (Devon), 45
Stour, River (Kent), 60
Stow, significance of, 88
Street patterns (urban), 71–3
Studies in Early English History, 37
Suffolk, 23, 40, 49, 54, 60, 66, 90, 114, 142–3
Sunderland (Co. Durham), 49
Surrey, 92
Surtees Society, *North Country Wills and Inventories*, 95
Sussex, 89
Swavesey (Cambs.), 62
Sysonby (Leics.), 82

Tavistock (Devon), 123
Tavistock Abbey (Finberg), 123 n.
Tax Assessments, 56
Techniques of Industrial Archaeology (Pannell), 12 n.
Teutonic School, harm done by, 78, 170
Thomson, T. R., 'The Early Bounds of Wanborough and Little Hinton', 39–40
Thomson, T. R., 'The Saxon Land Charters of Wiltshire', 36
Thornham (Norfolk), 63
Thorpe, Harry, *The Lord and the Landscape*, 76 n.
Thorverton (Devon), 98–9
Thurmaston (Leics.), 82
Timperley, H. W. *and* Brill, E., *Ancient Trackways of Wessex*, 137

Tithe Commutation Act, 1836, 113
Tithe maps and awards, 113
Tithe Redemption Commission, 113
'Tithe Surveys of the Mid-Nineteenth
    Century' (Prince), 113 n.
Torquay, History of (Russell), 72
Totnes (Devon), 28, 90
Towns, 65–73
Towns, exploration of, 24–9
Trackways, 136–8
Trees and shrubs, list of, 125–6
Trent and Mersey Canal, 11
Trowbridge (Wilts.), 69

Uppincott, Higher and Lower
    (Devon), 16
Urban housing, 67–71
Urban parish boundaries, 66

Vale of Evesham, 21
Vernacular building, 24 (*see also* Farm-
    steads, Houses, Urban housing)
Victoria County History of Leicestershire,
    70 n., 72
Victorian Suburb (Dyos), 71
Village Records (West), 95 n.
Villages, 73–6 and *passim* (*see also*
    Deserted villages)
Villein farms, 41–6

Walcott (Norfolk), 85
Wales and the Drovers (Hughes), 144 n.
Walls, 130–5
Walsingham (Norfolk), 63
Walton, significance of name, 87
Warborough Hill (Norfolk), 158
Ward, Gordon, 'A Roman colony near
    Brancaster', 142 n.
Ware (Herts.), 28–9
Warleggan parsonage (Cornwall),
    100–1
Warwickshire, 76 n., 88, 90
Watkins, Alfred, *The Old Straight
    Track*, 137

Waveney, River, 60
Waxham (Norfolk), 84
Welland Valley, Research Committee,
    174 n.
Wells (Norfolk), 63, 64
Welshpool (Salop), 60
West, John, *Village Records*, 95 n.
Weybourne (Norfolk), 63, 158–9
Whittington (Salop), 49
Widford (Oxon.), 86–7
Wigston Magna (Leics.), 46, 79, 80, 82,
    104, 115
Willan, T. S., *River Navigation in Eng-
    land*, 60 n.
Wiltshire, 36, 39–40, 69, 89, 91
Windmill Hill (Devon), 44
Wingham (Kent), 48–9
Winkleigh (Devon), 52
Winterton (Norfolk), 82–3
Wiscomb Park, Southleigh (Devon),
    52
Wiveton (Norfolk), 63, 151, 152, 153
Woodovis (Devon), 123
Woodstock (Oxon.), 92
Worcestershire, 34–5, 88
'Working class housing in Nottingham
    during the Industrial Revolution'
    (Chapman), 67 n.
Wormleighton (Warwicks.), 76 n.
Wreak, River (Leics.), 82
Wye, River, 60
Wyggeston Hospital Deeds, 46, 115
Wymondham (Leics.), 74
Wymondham (Norfolk), 27

Yare, River (Norfolk), 26, 33, 60
Yelland (Devon), 92
Yeo, River (Som.), 60
Yorkshire, 27, 60 n., 89, 92, 131–4,
    178–83
Youings, Joyce, *Devon Monastic Lands,
    Calendar of Particulars for Grants:
    1536–58*, 110 n.

Zeal Monachorum (Devon), 109, 110